SIBELIUS

OXFORD UNIVERSITY PRESS
AMEN HOUSE, E.C.4
LONDON   EDINBURGH   GLASGOW
NEW YORK TORONTO MELBOURNE
CAPETOWN   BOMBAY   CALCUTTA
MADRAS

HUMPHREY MILFORD
PUBLISHER TO THE
UNIVERSITY

Photograph by Ivar Helander, Helsinke-Helsingfors

JEAN SIBELIUS (1930)

SIBELIUS

By CECIL GRAY

Second Edition

HUMPHREY MILFORD

OXFORD UNIVERSITY PRESS
LONDON

First Edition	.	.	.	.	1931
Second Edition	.	.	.	.	1934
Second Impression		.	.	.	1938
Third Impression	.		.	:	1943
Fourth Impression		.	.	.	1945

Printed in Great Britain

To the
Finnish People
in sympathy
and
admiration

CONTENTS

PREFACE

FOR much of the biographical and other material information contained in the following pages I am indebted to the monograph on Sibelius written by his fellow-countryman Herr Erik Furuhjelm, in Swedish—'Jean Sibelius; hans tondiktning och drag ur hans liv' (Holger Schildts Förlag, Borga, 1916)—to which readers acquainted with that language are referred for fuller details. My thanks are also due to Sir Granville Bantock for his kind loan of the medal struck to commemorate Sibelius's fiftieth birthday, a reproduction of which is to be found on the cover of this book; and also to Mr. Norman Peterkin of the Oxford University Press for much valuable assistance of a practical kind.

C. G.

LONDON—HELSINGFORS—LONDON
1930–1

PART ONE
PRELIMINARIES

I. FOREWORD

THE doctrine that genius is always in advance of its age and that the great artist is seldom, if ever, recognized during his lifetime, was once believed to be an unchallengeable statement of fact. Until quite recently, indeed, the hostility or indifference of contemporaries was commonly assumed to be the necessary preliminary to the admiration of posterity, and the measure of an artist's greatness was almost deemed to be in direct ratio to the amount of abuse and opposition he succeeded in arousing. Corollarily, to achieve immediate success and popular recognition was in itself regarded as almost a proof positive of unworthiness.

Of late years, however, there has been a strong reaction against this conception of the great genius as a kind of Prometheus, bound to the rock of public indifference and neglect, and pecked at by the vulture of envious and malignant criticism. This, we are now assured, is a mere sentimental myth without the slightest basis or justification in historic fact. Mr. Ernest Newman, for example, in his book entitled *A Musical Critic's Holiday*, has been at pains to show that, so far as music at least is concerned, 'there has never yet been a composer so greatly in advance of his time that only an initiate here and there—one or two out of a vast population of cultivated musicians and music-lovers—could understand him'. On the contrary, Mr. Newman stoutly maintains, all the available evidence goes to show that the greatest composers in every age were recognized as such during their lifetimes, and invariably enjoyed the enthusiastic appreciation of their contemporaries.

Now, one can generally be fairly certain, whenever two such diametrically opposed views on a given subject exist, that firstly, each can point for support to a certain amount of solid and irrefutable evidence which the other deliberately ignores or attempts to explain away, and secondly, that neither of them, in the last resort, is valid. And so it is here. Certain great composers in the past have unquestionably been despised and rejected; equally undeniably others have received instant recognition and appreciation. Both phenomena, however, are in the nature of exceptions, and when they occur can usually be ascribed to extraneous and irrelevant circumstances connected with the personalities of the artists in question or with some abnormal conditions prevailing at the time, rather than to the intrinsic qualities of the works of art themselves, abstractly considered. Bach, for example, was largely ignored and neglected, not so much because he was a great composer as because his art belonged, both in spirit and in style, to a slightly earlier period than that in which he lived. His music, in fact, was not in accord with the prevailing *Zeitgeist*, and this is always fatal. If Beethoven must be conceded to have been, on the whole, appreciated by his contemporaries, it was because his music was in accord with the *Zeitgeist* of the period—not because he was a great composer, as is clearly and convincingly shown by the fact that what they really admired were not his best and most characteristic works such as the later string quartets, which they found completely baffling, not even the finest of the symphonies, which only enjoyed a modest *succès d'estime*, but the 'Septet', the 'Mount of Olives', and the 'Battle of Vittoria', which are amongst his feeblest productions and in no way superior to the work of countless other composers of his time.

The real facts of the matter, indeed, are neither so grandly and romantically tragic nor so reassuringly for the best in the best of all possible worlds as the one or the other theory would have us believe. The somewhat prosaic and unpalatable truth is that, exceptions apart, the greatest composers are as a rule neither vociferously acclaimed nor violently opposed, the reason being that the highest achievements in art are seldom the most immediately arresting or provocative. As that eminent French writer, M. André Gide, so admirably puts it, in his *Incidences*: 'J'estime que l'œuvre d'art accomplie sera celle qui passera d'abord inaperçue, qu'on ne remarquera même pas; où les qualités les plus contraires, les plus contradictoires en apparence: force et douceur, tenue et grâce, logique et abandon, précision et poésie — respireront si aisément qu'elles paraîtront naturelles et pas surprenantes du tout. Ce qui fait que le premier des renoncements à obtenir de soi c'est celui d'étonner ses contemporains.' And since the public in every age and clime demands to be astonished above all things, it follows naturally and inevitably that the artists who best minister to this desire and consequently attract the most immediate attention are neither the greatest nor even the smallest, but rather the novel, striking, picturesque, frequently original, always interesting, but essentially second-rate talents. It is they, as a general rule, who arouse the violent controversies and inspire all the wild enthusiasms and antagonisms, while the really great figures pass

comparatively unnoticed amidst a throng of medio-
crities.

No better illustration of the truth of the foregoing
observations could possibly be found than that
which is afforded by the subject of the present study.
It would certainly be untrue to say that Sibelius
has been neglected in the ordinary accepted sense
of the word. Rather the contrary, indeed; from one
point of view he might even legitimately be regarded
as one of the most popular of living composers, if
not the most popular of all without exception. His
name is a household word, as the saying is; 'Finlandia' is in the repertoire of every orchestra and
brass band, and 'Valse triste' is to be heard in
every picture-palace, restaurant, café, tea-shop, and
cabaret in the civilized world, from San Francisco
to Cairo, and from Stockholm to Capetown. At
the same time, however, the fact remains that the
great mass of his work, and certainly all that is best
of it, has been, up to the present time at least,
consistently and steadily ignored, with a quite
beautiful unanimity, by every section of the musical
community—executants, critics, and the public—
in every country in the world, apart from Finland,
and has only been appreciated by a few solitary
individuals here and there.

Some of the reasons for this state of affairs are readily discoverable and understandable. In the first place the music of Sibelius makes little or no appeal to conductors in general since it affords them few opportunities for indulging in choreographic displays or for exhibiting their own personalities, demanding instead a capacity for self-effacement and a degree of interpretative insight which few of them possess. It is not music which 'plays itself', as it were; unless the conductor, and through him the orchestra also, understand the music thoroughly, and are willing to devote long preparatory study and careful rehearsal to it, the result in performance is apt to be unsatisfactory and unconvincing. In a word, it is music which, without seeming difficult to the audience, is nevertheless exceedingly difficult to interpret—a most unalluring combination to conductors and orchestras whose natural desire is to exhibit their virtuosity at the least possible cost to themselves.

Secondly, Sibelius has been almost entirely ignored by critics up to the present time mainly because his music lacks to a great extent any strikingly noticeable stylistic features or methods of procedure which can be analysed, dissected, classified, pigeon-holed, and summed up in a trite and comprehensive formula. He exhibits no recognized modern tendency and belongs to no school, modal, atonal, polytonal, or any other; neither has he founded one of his own. He has nothing whatever in common with any of his contemporaries and he is also entirely uninfluenced by any of his immediate predecessors. He seems, in fact, to bear no relation to any other composer, past or present, and in consequence the ordinary historical-comparative methods of musical criticism are utterly useless in attempting to deal with him.

There are also certain material difficulties in the way of becoming acquainted with his work which must be taken into consideration. Not only are performances of his more important works exceedingly rare, for the reasons given above, but miniature scores of them—up to the time of writing— amount to no more than two in number, the Fifth Symphony and the String Quartet (*Voces Intimae*), op. 56.* It is, moreover, difficult to procure full scores of his other large works, or even the inevitably inadequate pianoforte arrangements of them, at musical circulating libraries or public institutions. Even the music section of the British Museum

---

* This remark and the subsequent ones are, fortunately, no longer true. (Note to 2nd Impression, 1938).

9

Reading-room possesses only the first three symphonies and a handful of miscellaneous works forming a selection so utterly unrepresentative and arbitrary that it is only charitable to suppose that they were chosen completely at random. The consequence is that in order to become familiar with Sibelius's work in its entirety it would be necessary for the ordinary student or critic to spend a sum of at least £50 or more in buying scores for himself. It is hardly surprising, perhaps, that very few would seem to have done so.

As for the musical public in general, the less said the better. On the rare occasions when one of Sibelius's major works has been performed the reception has invariably been sullen and listless. The 'plain man', indeed, whom Mr. Newman has appointed as arbiter of our destinies and proclaimed to be the sum and repository of all musical wisdom and virtue, simply will not listen to Sibelius at all—that is, to his best and most characteristic work.

The reason for this has already been suggested. The entire absence of sensationalism in this music, the deliberate renunciation of any attempt to 'étonner ses contemporains', inevitably renders it distasteful to audiences whose one desire is to be astonished at all costs. Sibelius himself summed up the position admirably when, according to his biographer Herr Furuhjelm, he once observed to a German music publisher to whom he brought his works that, whereas other modern composers were engaged in manufacturing cocktails of every hue and description, he offered the public pure cold water ('Här i utlandet fabricerar ni cocktails i olika kulörer, och nu kommer jag med rena källvattnet'). It is perhaps hardly to be expected that a generation whose aural palate has been vitiated and debauched by excessive indulgence in sonorous alcohol should take kindly to such an art as this. There is such a thing as the morning after, however—it has, indeed, already greyly dawned—and it is more than probable that in the immediate future audiences will find the pure cold water of Sibelius highly refreshing after the surfeit of musical cocktails in which they have been indulging so heavily and for so long. It is certainly true that within the last year or so signs have not been wanting of the commencement of a definite movement in favour of Sibelius in England, and its eventual spread to other countries can only be a matter of time.

Enlightened musical opinion here, in fact, contrary to the generally accepted notion, is much more alert and discriminating, and actually, though perhaps not apparently, more advanced even, in the conventional sense of the word, than in any other large European country at the present time. In Germany, France, Italy, the national art invariably enjoys preferential treatment. They have all established a kind of spiritual *douane*, a tariff wall through which foreign musical imports are only able to penetrate in the form of mere fashionable curiosities, *articles de luxe* for the delectation of the snobbish few. In the long run only German music is freely welcomed in Germany, only French music in France, only Italian music in Italy. In England, on the other hand, we have been musically as well as economically free-traders; not being self-supporting, we have opened our doors to works of every nationality without favour or prejudice. And while it may well be true that our policy of free imports has acted as a powerful deterrent to the cultivation of a national art comparable to that which can be found in 'protected' countries, at the same time it has certainly conduced to the formation of a more enlightened, eclectic, and impartial body of critical opinion than is possible elsewhere. And the fact that the art of Sibelius is, at long last, beginning to be appreciated here at its proper value is, I think, a highly significant portent for the immediate future.

But let there be no mistake about it; the degree
of recognition and appreciation with which it has
hitherto met, even in this country, is ludicrously
and disproportionately small in comparison with the
amount lavished on many second-rate talents in
the musical world at the present time, and reflects
the utmost discredit on all concerned.[1] Conductors,
critics, publishers, executants of every kind, the
public in general—all are equally guilty of having
disgracefully ignored and neglected the composer
who, I am convinced, will ultimately prove to have
been, not only the greatest of his generation, but
one of the major figures in the entire history of music.

Such an extreme and challenging statement, I am
well aware, is likely to arouse a considerable amount
of surprise, dissent, and even derision in certain
quarters. I can only say that it is made with all due
deliberation, as the result of a steadily growing con-
viction which has been in the course of formation
over a period of many years, and that it is at least
based upon a more prolonged and exhaustive study
of the music than is likely to have been made by
any of those who question it. Above all, it is no
mere expression of a personal predilection; rather
is it true that I have been forced to it, almost against

[1] From this general stricture I would exempt his native country.

13

my will and in spite of myself. One after another the more immediately arresting and spectacular figures of the present time engaged my attention and aroused my interest and enthusiasm; one after another they gradually ceased in the last resort to satisfy and hold me, while all the time the figure of Sibelius gradually and imperceptibly grew in stature and significance until now he overshadows them all. Such at any rate has been my own personal experience, and such, I firmly believe, will prove to be the experience of all intelligent musicians and music-lovers who are sufficiently acquainted with his work to be able to judge for themselves. If this little book should be the means of inducing a few to make the effort to become so acquainted, its modest purpose will have been achieved.

II. THE BACKGROUND

THE question of nationality in music is one of the most wearisome and least profitable of all possible subjects of aesthetic discussion, and probably the one on which most nonsense has been talked and written. It will be necessary, however, to touch briefly upon this well-worn topic in order to dispel certain misconceptions which have grown up around Sibelius and his art.

Nationalism in music may be said to be of two kinds. In the one a specific regional character is deliberately and consciously cultivated by means of the employment of folk-songs as thematic material, or by the concoction of idioms largely based upon the peculiarities to be found in them; in the other it is wholly unconscious and unintentional, the outcome of environment or tradition, latent in the basic thought rather than in the outward style, a thing one can neither cultivate nor rid oneself of even if one would. The former is essentially a product of the nineteenth century, an offshoot of the romantic movement; the latter has always existed to some extent or other. Examples of the first type are to be found in the music of the

Russian group of The Five, or in that of Smetana, Grieg, de Falla, Bartók, and Kodály, while most other composers betray some degree of nationalism of the second variety. For example, it would obviously be impossible to deny that Palestrina and Monteverde, however different their externals may be, are both nevertheless profoundly Italian, and Bach and Beethoven profoundly German, at bottom.

Sibelius, largely as a result of the immense vogue and popularity of a small and unimportant work, 'Finlandia', has generally been regarded as a member of the first group, and the characteristics and idiosyncrasies of his art have been commonly ascribed to the supposedly racial source of his inspiration and to the idiomatic peculiarities of the folk-music of his native land. Dr. Walter Niemann, for example, in his little book on Sibelius, says that his art is 'der musikalische Ausdruck der finnischen Volksseele' ('the musical expression of the Finnish folk-soul'), and in many other passages too numerous to quote here, gives the reader to understand that his style is largely based upon the idioms of Finnish folk-songs.

This is a complete misconception. It cannot be too strongly emphasized at the outset that Sibelius is not, and never has been, a nationalist composer in the narrow sense in which the words are generally used. In the first place he has never once, so far as I am, or he is, aware, made use of a folk-song in any of his compositions. It is true that he has arranged a small group of Finnish melodies for pianoforte, but that is a very different thing from using them as material for his own works. The fact, moreover, that these arrangements are published without opus number suggests that the composer does not regard them as his own work, strictly speaking. Apart from them there is a small quantity of music, chiefly for unaccompanied chorus, such as the part-songs, op. 15, and the Cantata for the year 1897, op. 23, in which certain traces can be perceived of the stylistic features of Finnish folk-music. These works, however, admirable though they may be in many ways (the Cantata in particular), constitute such a minute proportion of the composer's immense output that they cannot be regarded as being in any way characteristic or representative.

For the rest it is virtually impossible, save for an occasional phrase here and there, to find any traces of nationalism whatsoever, in the generally accepted sense of the word, in the music of Sibelius. The alleged nationalism of 'Finlandia' itself, for example, lies exclusively in its title. It is safe to say that no one listening to it without the preconceptions induced thereby would find anything specifically Finnish about it at all. The work may conceivably have been inspired by patriotic sentiments, but that is a very different thing. Not merely are the themes the composer's own, but they are in no way imitations of the national folk-music, as they are invariably represented to be. One frequently finds it said in concert programme notes, for example, that the themes in 'Finlandia' are such close copies of Finnish folk-songs that it is difficult to believe that they are not authentic specimens—a statement so manifestly absurd that it could only be made by writers who know nothing whatever about Finnish folk-music. I remember once mentioning this seemingly authoritative statement to the composer and expressing my surprise and perplexity at it, in that I had inspected a considerable quantity of Finnish folk-songs without ever coming across a single one bearing any resemblance to the themes in this work. I was relieved and amused to discover that he was equally at a loss to indicate the models on which he was alleged to have based them, and equally unable to discover the slightest traces of any national element whatsoever in the music, except possibly general sentiment of the vaguest kind as indicated by the title.

Niemann, again, professes to find in Finnish folk-song the source of the thematic material of Sibelius's symphonies, which he proceeds to criticize adversely on that account, declaring that folk-song material is unsuited to symphonic treatment—a view with which one can only cordially concur, subject to the important qualification that the symphonies of Sibelius make no use whatsoever of folk-songs or even of themes modelled on them, and apart from an occasional phrase or two in the first of the series, which have a slightly Finnish flavour, betray no national characteristics at all in the accepted sense of the word.

We shall have occasion to deal more fully with this preposterous suggestion elsewhere; for the present it is enough to say that these and similar misstatements by Niemann and others have led to the establishment of a totally wrong conception of Sibelius in the mind of the musical public.

Incidentally, while we are on the subject of Finnish folk-music it might be as well to say that, apart from a relatively small group distinguished by the employment of a characteristic kind of 5/4—and more occasionally 7/4—rhythm, and a tendency to restrict the melodic compass to the interval of a fifth or so, Finnish folk-song is on the whole rather lacking in any strongly marked national peculiarities. Indeed, the majority of the indisputably authentic and ancient examples of it which have been recorded have much the same characteristics as Gregorian chant, from which they undoubtedly derive; while the more modern examples are of the rather indeterminate and eclectic type encountered in Scandinavian, and more particularly Swedish, folk-music, from which they in their turn also undoubtedly derive. Paradoxically enough, therefore, if Sibelius had really built upon Finnish folk-songs as his melodic basis, his work would be much more conventional and colourless in style than it actually is, and even less distinctively national in all probability. For it would be idle to deny that his art is in a sense profoundly national; it is national, however, in the second of the two ways defined above. In other words, Sibelius is a Finnish composer in precisely the same way and to precisely the same extent that Richard Strauss, say, is a German composer or Sir Edward Elgar an English composer, but that is all. The fact that Strauss sets German subjects and texts to music, and Elgar English ones, does not seem to us particularly remarkable or cause us to search for a non-existent local colour in their music, but when Sibelius sets Finnish poetry to music or seeks inspiration in the national epic, the *Kalevala*, people at once begin to imagine that what are in reality the individual qualities of the composer's mind and method of working are only explicable as being the outcome of some exotic national characteristics. This is the mistake which must be guarded against.

If the national element, then, in the music of Sibelius is of no more importance than the German element in that of Strauss or the English element in that of Elgar it is at the same time of no less importance. We are inclined to under-estimate the degree of nationalism in the two latter as much as we are inclined to over-estimate it in the former simply because we happen to be so familiar with both German and English musical traditions and culture in general that we do not notice it or think about it at all. And while it is true that Sibelius would have been just as great a composer if he had been born in Germany or England instead of Finland, he would undoubtedly have been a different one. In short, it is certainly possible to appreciate the art of Sibelius without any reference whatever to his geographical provenance or cultural traditions, but we shall probably understand it better, more completely, if we have some slight knowledge of them—it need be no more than that. I can only say from personal experience that although my opinion of his music was as high a one before I became acquainted with its antecedents as it was after, a knowledge of them, imperfect and superficial though it admittedly is, has helped me to understand and appreciate certain aspects of his work which I might not otherwise have done, and to perceive nuances and subtleties in it which might else have escaped me.

I propose, therefore, before giving an account of the man and his work, to attempt to give a slight idea or impression of the cultural background from which they emerge; for if, as it is reasonable to assume, my readers' ignorance of Finland and things Finnish is as complete as mine was until quite recently, they should find it useful, despite its manifest sketchiness and inadequacy, for which I offer all due apologies.

To begin with, for example, the hazy conception that most people in south-western Europe have of Finland is that of a desolate wilderness enveloped in perennial ice and snow, and sparsely inhabited by Eskimos or some equally uncouth and primitive

race which subsists chiefly upon a diet of whale-
blubber and pemmican, and ekes out a dreary and
precarious existence by bartering furs and hides
with traders in exchange for the bare necessities of
life. To those many people it will doubtless come
as a surprise to learn that Finland, despite its
northern latitude and eastern longitude, is nevertheless a highly civilized country. Statistics show that
as far back as 1900 no more than 1·2 per cent. of the
population was illiterate—a record of which no
other country in the world could boast at that time
—and since then this minute percentage has
dwindled into nothing. The general level of educa-
tion, moreover, is unusually high, and the ratio of
widely cultured individuals to the community is
probably greater in Finland than anywhere else at
the present day. Her political constitution is the
last word in enlightened democracy, and she was
the first European country to introduce woman
suffrage—also, incidentally, to experience the con-
jectural benefits and dubious delights of Prohibition.

Needless to say, I am far from wishing to suggest
that all these features are necessarily admirable or
desirable in themselves. My only purpose in mentioning these rather intimate sociological details is to
show that Finland, so far from being the backward

23

and uncivilized country that she is popularly supposed to be, is on the contrary one of the most—if not, indeed, as is very probable, quite the most—advanced and progressive country in Europe to-day. And when we take into consideration the façt that the entire population amounts to less than half that of London alone—a mere three million or so—it is certainly not going too far to say that the Finnish achievement in almost every branch of artistic, scientific, sociological, and political activity is truly impressive and almost without parallel. For example, the modern school of architecture would seem to have had its origin there, and at least three of its exponents—Saarinen, Sonck, and Lindgren—are among the foremost living practitioners of the art; in music she can claim, in addition to the subject of the present book, at least four names known to all concert-goers, if not, perhaps, of the first rank—Järnefelt, Merikanto, Palmgren, and Melartin; while in literature, sculpture, and painting she can more than hold her own with other countries of greater size, even if little of it has as yet achieved a European reputation.

It is important that this should be recognized, for the erroneous impression, so widely spread, to the effect that the Baltic countries are a kind of northern equivalent of the Balkans, in which Finland occupies much the same obscure and lowly position that Albania does in the latter, is primarily responsible for many misunderstandings concerning the art of Sibelius, and above all, for the totally unwarranted attitude of patronizing condescension which ill-informed critics have frequently seen fit to adopt towards it. For example, it has been responsible for the tendency to regard his work, and to dismiss it slightingly, as 'primitive', whereas it is for the most part exceedingly subtle and refined, both in thought and style. Again, many who would be prepared to concede that a composer belonging to such an uncultured country as they wrongly suppose Finland to be might conceivably entertain or edify us by his exploitation of some quaint and exotic form of local colour, some specifically and exclusively national train of thought, are nevertheless disinclined to acknowledge the possibility that he might be able to handle, as to the manner born, the great classical forms which they are jealously disposed to regard as the exclusive apanage and inalienable prerogative of the larger and more 'civilized' European countries.

This attitude of mind is, of course, peculiarly prevalent in Germany, whose critics are even unwilling to admit that a composer belonging to any other country but their own could possibly write a tolerably good symphony—not even an Englishman, a Frenchman, or an Italian, let alone a mere Finn. This attitude clearly underlies all German criticisms of Sibelius's symphonies, and is primarily accountable for the way in which they are contemptuously ignored or dismissed as negligible in Teutonic countries. The remark of Dr. Niemann which we have already quoted is by no means an isolated case. One finds exactly the same thing in the late Dr. Weissmann's book, *Some Problems of Modern Music*, where he says that Sibelius 'was caught in the toils of local colour and found it difficult to attain symphonic form', and again that he is 'preoccupied with Western Impressionism which colours his graphic, lyrical, and very national music and prevents him from doing great symphonic work'—all of which is absolutely and entirely untrue.

Conversely, those for whom startling novelty and reckless experimentation are the most desirable attributes in a modern composer consider Sibelius's comparatively restrained and traditional style of writing to be merely old-fashioned in consequence of his belonging to what they fondly imagine to be a backward and primitive race beyond the pale of civilization and at least a century behind the times. The truth is precisely the opposite, namely, that Sibelius—as I hope to be able to show in the course of this study—can be as daring and original in his procedure as any one when it happens to suit his aesthetic purpose. And if it is true that he does not share in the contemporary love of experimentation for its own sake—which is only a phase that is already passing—the reason is not that he is behind the times but rather that he is ahead of them, in the same way that Finland is, in many ways at least, ahead of other European countries.

One's first impression, indeed, on arriving at Helsingfors—or Helsinki, as it is called in the vernacular—is that one has been magically transported not so much to a new country as to a new age; as if one had been travelling through time rather than through space upon the fabulous machine imagined by H. G. Wells in one of his early romances. So far from being a mere collection of log-cabins and ice-huts, as most people probably suppose, Helsingfors is, on the contrary, one of the most modern and up-to-date cities in Europe, in comparison with which London or Paris seem—and are—in many respects backward and old-fashioned.

This impression of extreme modernity is particularly intensified if one happens to cross over from Reval—or Tallinn as it is now called—the capital of the newly created republic of Esthonia, some fifty miles away on the opposite side of the Gulf of Finland. Reval, an old Hanseatic town, with its narrow, winding, cobbled streets, its ancient city-walls, gates, and battlements, its Byzantine cupolas and minarets, its red-roofed gabled houses huddled together in picturesque confusion, belongs wholly to the past; it is a crazy compendium and epitome of medieval European history, a palimpsest in stone on which Danes, Swedes, Teutonic Knights, Russians, Poles, Lithuanians, and others have all left traces of their passage during the course of a thousand years of varied and troubled history. Helsingfors, on the contrary, with its spacious, well-planned streets laid out for the most part symmetrically at right angles to each other, and lined with large and sumptuous buildings designed in an aggressively modernistic style of architecture, is almost wholly the creation of recent times: with no past to speak of, but with an intensely vital present, and a future of even greater promise. One might almost say that there is something non-European and transatlantic in its newness and spick-and-span modernity were it not for the fact that it exudes a curiously strong and vivid individuality which differentiates it as sharply from the uniform and characterless mushroom growths of the New World as it does from the mature and historic cities of the Old. Helsingfors, indeed, is a city quite *sui generis*, with an atmosphere and character so peculiarly its own that it is difficult to compare it with any other, or to define its individuality by any known analogy.

This quality of utter difference from everywhere else, this curious sense of 'otherness', as D. H. Lawrence would say, is the distinctive feature, not only of the capital, but of the whole country, its people, their art, their entire culture. Finland, indeed, with her countless lakes, islands, and illimitable forests, together covering no less than nine-tenths of the area of the country; with her desolate moors strewn with granite boulders sometimes as large as houses, sometimes suggesting by their fantastic shapes huge carvings such as those of Easter Island, made by some extinct race of giants— Finland is unlike any other country in the world; and her strange physique is allied to a climatic temperament of violent extremes, ranging from a bitter arctic cold in winter to a fierce tropic heat in summer.

The inhabitants of this singular country are themselves equally singular, both ethnologically and linguistically. Their very origin is wrapped in impenetrable mystery. Situated between Scandinavian peoples on the one side and Slavonic peoples on the other, the Finns are sharply differentiated from both alike, and indeed from all other races in Europe with the possible exception of the Magyars, to whom they are supposed to be related, though only remotely. Their language, too, both in vocabulary and methods of grammatical construction, is totally dissimilar to that of any other people save the Esthonians, who, however, are only a minor branch of the same race. And although it is true that a certain admixture of blood took place during the long period (1157–1808) when Finland was under Swedish rule, particularly in the larger towns in the south, the racial characteristics of the people remained fundamentally unaltered, and the subsequent century and more of Russian domination, culminating in a period of fierce oppression, only served to intensify their strongly national consciousness.

Finland, in fact, may only have been independent politically since the Russian revolution of 1917, but spiritually she has never been anything else. The fact that Finnish culture is to some extent Swedish means no more than that Irish culture is to a great extent English. Indeed, the parallel is in many respects a very close one, for in the same way and for the same reasons that the greatest Irish writers have always employed English as their medium of expression without thereby sacrificing anything of their intensely nationalistic outlook, so in the past the leading Finnish authors wrote mainly in Swedish. In recent times, however, and more especially since the attainment of independence in both countries, there has been a common tendency to employ the native language as the medium for literary expression; and in the same way that in their endeavour to create a national literature the Irish writers of the so-called Celtic Renaissance turned to their ancient myths and legends, so Finnish artists have frequently sought inspiration in their great national epic, the *Kalevala*. Since a considerable number of Sibelius's works, particularly of his earlier period, are based upon or indirectly connected with this poem, it will perhaps be as well to say a few words about it here.

In the first half of the nineteenth century Elias Lönnrot, the son of a poor village tailor, inspired probably by the example of Macpherson's 'Ossian', the fame of which had spread throughout Europe, conceived the idea of compiling a similar epic poem out of the materials afforded by Finnish folk-poetry and mythology. But whatever the truth may be concerning the genuineness or the reverse of its Gaelic prototype there can be no question whatever concerning the authenticity of the *Kalevala*. All that Lönnrot did was to combine in one version the best elements of several versions, to arrange the disjointed episodes in a more or less coherent sequence, and to provide the links between them whenever necessary. The first edition appeared in 1835, the second, considerably enlarged and revised, in 1849. Two English translations have been published, by J. M. Crawford and W. F. Kirby respectively. That of the latter, which is obtainable in the 'Everyman' series, is the version I have used for all necessary quotations that occur in the course of this book.

The poem, which is written in the distinctive metre taken over by Longfellow and used in his *Hiawatha*, relates the deeds and adventures of four principal heroes; Väinämöinen, the Orpheus of Finnish mythology, and a powerful magician; Ilmarinen, his brother, a cunning artificer and smith; Lemminkäinen, a kind of northern Don Juan; and

Kullervo, a strange, sombre figure whose tragic destiny recalls that of Oedipus. The principal heroines are also four in number; Ilmatar, Daughter of the Air and mother of Väinämöinen; Aino, his beloved; Louhi, Mistress of the Northland; and her comely daughter the Maid of Pohjola, who becomes the wife of Ilmarinen.

It would take too long if I were to attempt to give here a detailed résumé of the contents of the fifty *runos*, or cantos as we should call them, which comprise the poem. The various episodes with which the reader should be acquainted in order to understand those works of Sibelius which are based upon them will be described later, in their proper place together with the music. For the present it is enough to indicate the more salient characteristics of this remarkable folk-epos, which are, firstly, a strong feeling for nature and, secondly, a pre-occupation with magic, both of which play a more prominent role in the *Kalevala* than in any other ancient literature in the world.

All the poetry of the Finns, indeed, has its origin in magical incantations, and as Comparetti says in the erudite study he has devoted to the *Kalevala*, 'magic makes itself felt among the Finns in every circumstance of material and intellectual life'. From

D

33

the earliest times, moreover, the Finns have always had the reputation amongst their neighbours of being adepts in the black arts. The wizards encountered in Scandinavian mythology and folk-lore are almost invariably said to be Finnish, and the practice of resorting to members of that race in order to acquire their magic arts became so prevalent during the Middle Ages that the Church found it necessary to enact laws forbidding it.

An interesting illustration of their widespread reputation for magical powers is to be found in an ancient Scottish ballad which narrates how

> A Finn cam ower fra Norroway
> Fir ta pit töthache away,

and even in modern times it was commonly believed by sailors that the Finn had the power of conjuring up storms and tempests, and also of providing favourable winds at will. Even to-day, we are told, 'British sailors have a strong aversion to sailing with a Finn as a member of the crew. They believe that he is a wizard with uncanny powers. It is not only that he can stick his knife into the mast and extract a tot of rum'—one fails to see why British sailors should have a strong aversion to that —'but he can command the elements, he holds commerce with unseen powers, he is an adept at black magic'.[1]

Without going so far as to suggest that these allegations are strictly true, both in substance and in liquid, I think it can nevertheless be safely said that no popular belief of this kind, so widespread and so longstanding, can be entirely without some kind of foundation. It is no doubt due, in part at least, to an instinctive recognition on the part of the common people of the separateness and isolation of the Finnish race in Europe, to which ethnology attests. The 'mysterious stranger' in any community is always suspected of commerce with the black arts, and the Finn is certainly felt to be different from themselves by all neighbouring races. But there is more in it than that. The preoccupation with magic which is to be found in the *Kalevala*, and the reputation for magical powers which has clung so persistently to the Finnish race throughout history, from the earliest times up to the present day, aptly symbolize a definite aspect of the national mentality which comes out very strongly in their art—a fantastic, eerie, and slightly sinister quality of imagination which is quite characteristic and unmistakable. As Mr. MacCallum Scott truly says

[1] A. MacCallum Scott, *Through Finland to St. Petersburg.*

in his admirable book, *Suomi: The Land of the Finns*, 'Finnish literature, painting, architecture, music, are alike conscious that they have their roots in ancient magic'.

One feels it particularly strongly in the new architecture, in the strange and menacing Berghälls Kyrka of Lars Sonck, for example, which rears its head over Helsingfors like a hooded snake about to strike, and in innumerable other buildings which give the city its peculiar stamp and atmosphere. 'Magic,' too, it is interesting to note, is the word which recurs most frequently, like a *leitmotiv*, in all attempts of travellers to define the peculiar impression which the country itself makes upon one; the magic of the long winters when nature lies as if spell-bound under its shroud of snow, and the flickering ribbons of the Northern Lights are blown about the sky; the magic of the sudden awakening of spring, when the earth throws off its icy fetters and the buds leap from their sheaths, as if at the stroke of an enchanter's wand; the magic of the long days and white nights of summer, when the earth has barely time to cool and the vegetation grows with miraculous rapidity, in tropical profusion; the magic of autumn, when the great gales blow in from the Baltic with demoniac intensity, bringing rain-laden clouds which darken the sky as they approach, like the outspread wings of some fabulous giant-bird in the Arabian Nights. The whole feeling of the country, in fact, its landscape and scenery, its climate, its inhabitants, their art and culture in general—all have a strange, indefinable quality about them for which one can find no other word than magic—Finnish magic.

The reader is now in a position to estimate for himself the extent to which the peculiar characteristics of the art of Sibelius are due to national conditions and cultural circumstances, and to what extent they are purely personal. The almost aggressive modernity that is so typical of Finland to-day is certainly not to be found in his work; indeed, its comparative sobriety and conservatism might be plausibly accounted for as the outcome of a strong reaction against environment. On the other hand the intense love of nature, which is such a dominating trait of the national genius, is exceptionally highly developed in Sibelius. In no music of modern times, in fact, save possibly in that of Delius, does one feel it so deeply and unmistakably. As Herr Oscar Andersson says in a study of Sibelius's music published in a French collection of essays dealing with Finland (*Finlande et Finlandais*, 1913), 'de tous les compositeurs actuels il est peut-être le plus grand admirateur de la nature', and in his art 'les images visuelles se transforment en images musicales'. Finally, the magical quality which is so characteristic a feature of the national art of all kinds comes out particularly strongly in that of Sibelius—not merely by virtue of the strain of fantastic and eerie imagination which one encounters so often in the works based upon national subjects, but also by the way in which he succeeds in imbuing the most ordinary and even commonplace progressions, especially in his later works, with a profound meaning and significance for which there is no adequate word but 'magical', for it triumphantly defies any attempt at analysis or rational explanation.

III. THE MAN

BIOGRAPHICAL notices concerning Sibelius in works of reference invariably open with two flagrant misstatements: firstly, that he is of purely Finnish extraction, and, secondly, that he comes of peasant stock. I have before me as I write a genealogical table published in the Finnish periodical 'Aulos' which shows that, out of the thirty-two direct ancestors of Sibelius living about 1700, eighteen were Finnish Swedes—i.e. persons of Swedish origin living in Finland—nine were pure Swedes, and one was German, leaving only four pure Finns. So far as blood and race go, therefore, Sibelius is predominantly, even overwhelmingly, Swedish, not Finnish. He does not himself attach much importance to the fact, however, being of the opinion that environment and tradition are much more actively formative of national characteristics than are racial origins, which are seldom, if ever, pure. In any case the Swedes in Finland have become so closely assimilated to the indigenous population as to be virtually indistinguishable from it save in the overheated imaginations of the more extreme Finnish Chauvinists.

As regards the second point, this genealogical table also shows that the majority of his ancestors were clergymen, doctors, merchants, small landowners, and so forth, and that of the remainder none was a peasant in the strict sense of the word, their social status being perhaps best represented by our old English word 'yeoman' as defined in dictionaries—i.e. 'a member of a class of small freeholders, forming the next grade below gentlemen, a man of small estate, any small farmer or countryman above the grade of labourer'. In other words Sibelius, in common with the vast majority of eminent artists, springs from what we vaguely term the middle classes, or *bourgeoisie*.

This is a point of much greater importance than that of racial origin, not for any snobbish reasons, but simply because the idea of Sibelius which the legend of his peasant ancestry encourages is apt to be somewhat misleading. Much of the talk concerning the alleged primitivism of his music, in fact, to which I have already alluded, can be traced to this preconceived notion that he is a hornyhanded son of the soil, a kind of semi-illiterate, self-educated, natural genius, expressing himself awkwardly in a quaint musical vernacular. The truth is that with few exceptions his ancestors were persons possessing a high degree of culture and refinement.

None of them, it would seem, was ever a musician or an artist of any kind by vocation, but several, particularly, on his mother's side, were musical amateurs of considerable distinction. His great grandfather, for example, a Dr. Mathias Åkerberg, was a 'cellist of no mean ability, and most of the composer's immediate ancestors appear to have practised the art in one way or another. A certain streak of fantasy, moreover, crops up at irregular intervals in the family records, and believers in heredity may perhaps find the explanation of Sibelius's talent in the accidental combination of this sporadic trait with the fairly constant inclination towards music which the family displayed. Of truly outstanding ability in any direction, however, there is little trace amongst his progenitors.

Jean (Johan) Julius Christian Sibelius was born on the 8th of December 1865 at Tavastehus, a smallish town in the interior of Finland, where his father, Christian Gustav Sibelius, pursued the calling of regimental doctor. He does not appear to have been an exceptional child in any way, certainly not an infant prodigy. For the most part his tastes and inclinations were those of all normal boys. It is

41

true that at an early age he was in the habit of improvising at the piano, but then probably most children are if there is an instrument at hand, in the same way that most children attempt to draw even if they have no special talent for it. Regular instruction in piano playing did not begin until he was nine years old, and about the same time he would seem to have begun to compose systematically. A small piece for violin and 'cello, *pizzicato*, called 'Waterdrops', dating from this time, has been preserved, and shows a sense of style and a degree of craftsmanship which are certainly unusual at such an early age, but hardly sufficiently so to warrant the appellation of genius, even in embryo. The modest technical competence, indeed, which it reveals, is more commonly found in association with a minor talent than with any genuinely creative urge, which, in its earliest phases, is generally inclined to be clumsy and inarticulate rather than facile and accomplished.

The first faint stirrings of something more than mere technical aptitude would seem to date back no earlier than his fifteenth year, when he began to take violin lessons from the military bandmaster of the town, Gustav Levander. During the summer months, we are told by Herr Furuhjelm, he would often spend entire days and nights out in the woods or by the side of the neighbouring lake of Vana-javesi, one of the loveliest spots in Finland, improvising endlessly on his violin in an attempt to reproduce in music the emotions aroused in him by the beauties of nature.

About the same time he began to play the violin in the school orchestra and to take part in chamber music *ensembles* with his brother Christian (now professor of psychiatry at the University of Helsing-fors) and his sister Linda, who played the 'cello and the piano respectively. In this way he laid the foundations of the deep knowledge and love of the classics and the intimate understanding of the nature and capacities of the stringed instrume ts which were destined to exercise such an important influence on the unfolding of his creative powers.

His violin master, incidentally, had in addition given him some lessons in musical theory, but for the most part his knowledge of the principles of composition was self-acquired through incessant practice, supplemented by an exhaustive study of Marx's *Kompositionslehre*. During the years 1880–5 he was exceptionally active in the field of chamber music, and works written in this period which still survive in manuscript include a trio in A minor, a piano quartet in E minor, a string quartet in E flat, a sonata for piano and violin in D minor, an andantino for 'cello in C, and a string trio fragment in G minor.

Despite the exceptional promise revealed in these early works the idea of becoming a musician was considered quite out of the question. Never, even under the most favourable circumstances, a calling which appeals strongly to parents as a possible means of livelihood for their offspring, the profession of music in Finland at that time was a more than usually precarious one. Consequently it was decided that Sibelius should take up the law, and after matriculating in May 1885 he embarked upon a course of jurisprudence at the University in Helsingfors. A short time later, however, after vainly attempting to combine the study of the law with that of music, which he simultaneously pursued under Martin Wegelius at the Music Institute, Sibelius definitely abandoned the former and henceforth devoted himself entirely to his art.

Martin Wegelius seems, by a happy chance, to have been an ideal teacher. From a pedagogue pure and simple the student can learn nothing of value that he could not get just as well from a book; from an accomplished composer, on the other hand, he is apt to learn too much, and to become merely an imperfect echo of his master. Wegelius belonged to neither of these categories. He was a strict disciplinarian without being a pedant, and enough of a composer himself to be of practical assistance in helping to solve the many problems that arise in the early stages of creative activity, without being a sufficiently powerful or original one to exercise an undue influence over the student's personality.

It is true that he did not altogether recognize the exceptional nature of his pupil's talents. Sibelius himself has said that Wegelius was like a father to him, but that he did not entirely approve of his more individual works—but there is nothing very surprising in that. Indeed, it is only natural that it should be so. Genuine originality in the course of formation is not always easily distinguishable from the striving after it. It is only when we look back from a master's mature works to his early ones that we find the first traces of a personal quality significant and attractive. At the time, without this foreknowledge, they might very easily seem to be precisely the opposite.

The methods of instruction followed at Helsingfors would seem to have compared more than favourably with those at most other conservatoires in the 'eighties, when the closest adherence to what was fondly imagined to be the strict church style (but was actually nothing of the kind) was still rigorously and universally enjoined. Wegelius, on the contrary, required his students to alternate between exercises in the strictest scholastic style and spells of entirely free composition. This is probably the ideal method of training, for although the old system, now utterly discredited and for the most part abandoned, is admittedly of no immediate practical use in teaching one how to compose, it is of considerable indirect benefit, not merely as a form of mental discipline, but also in a way that it is impossible to define. It is exceedingly difficult, in fact, to say in what precisely its value consists; one only knows that those composers who have not gone through the old academic curriculum invariably seem to lack something essential.

Works written during this period of apprenticeship comprise a theme and variations in C minor for string quartet, with which Sibelius made his first public appearance as a composer, a sonata in F major for violin and piano, a trio for strings, a suite in A major for string trio in five movements, two string quartets in A minor and B flat major respectively, and a melodrama, 'Svartjukans nätter', for recitation, singing voice, piano, violin, and 'cello, to words of Runeberg. At the same time Sibelius continued to study the violin, under Wasilieff and Csillag, playing second fiddle in the string quartet of the Institute and eventually acquiring sufficient proficiency on the instrument to be able to perform the solo part of Mendelssohn's concerto creditably in public.

During these student days, it is interesting to note, Sibelius became acquainted with Ferruccio Busoni, who was then acting as professor of the piano at the Music Institute in Helsingfors. A warm friendship grew up between the two young men which was later to bear fruit in the enthusiastic propagandist campaign conducted by Busoni on his friend's behalf in Germany.

In the autumn of 1889 Sibelius left his native country for the first time in order to work under Albert Becker in Berlin. His studies there were mainly contrapuntal, and he wrote a large quantity of vocal and instrumental fugues about this time, while continuing his violinistic activities under Sachse and Struss. In comparison both with foregoing and subsequent periods, however, Sibelius's stay in Berlin was somewhat unproductive, the only work of any size or importance written during this year being a piano quintet in G minor. A certain antagonism between master and pupil, the glamour and social distractions of a great European capital experienced for the first time, the sudden revelation, after a strictly classical training, of the most recent and spectacular achievements in modern musical art—Strauss's 'Don Juan', for example, which he heard then for the first time, must have made a deep impression on him—all these factors no doubt contributed something towards this momentary pause in his productivity. About the same period, moreover, he became engaged to, and subsequently married, Aino, daughter of General August Alexander Järnefelt, a name illustrious in both Russian and Finnish annals: in the first on account of the number of distinguished soldiers, and in the second on account of the number of eminent artists, who have borne it. Three brothers of Madame Sibelius, for example, are poet, painter, and musician respectively, all of exceptional talent. The latter, Armas Järnefelt, is at present the musical director of the opera at Stockholm, and the composer of the well-known 'Praeludium' and other works.

After spending about a year in Berlin Sibelius left for Vienna, where he studied under Carl

Goldmark and Robert Fuchs. He frequented musical circles and became acquainted with, amongst others, Brahms, who expressed a highly favourable opinion on some songs of Sibelius which had been brought to his notice—an unusual gesture, by the way, on the part of Brahms, who can hardly be said to have been conspicuous exactly for his sympathetic and encouraging attitude towards unknown young composers. Besides these songs—presumably the 'Seven Songs of Runeberg', subsequently published as op. 13,—Sibelius wrote here an octet for flute, clarinet, and strings which, I understand (though I have not seen it), contained the germ of the later 'En Saga', and also his first two orchestral works, an 'Overture in E major' and 'Balettscen', besides sketches for his first great work, 'Kullervo'.

In the meanwhile the works he had been writing had been played in Finland with conspicuous success, and by the time he returned to his native country in 1892 he already enjoyed a considerable reputation which was crowned by the first performance on the 28th of April in that year of his recently completed symphony for soloists, chorus, and orchestra, 'Kullervo'. After a few years during which he taught composition and the violin at the Music Institute in Helsingfors, he was accorded a

E

modest stipend or life-grant by the Finnish government which enabled him to relinquish his uncongenial teaching activities and to devote himself henceforth entirely to composition.

Such a generous and enlightened policy on the part of a government towards a young artist must be wellnigh unique in modern times, and deserves every praise. It must be admitted, however, that there are certain risks attached to such a well-meaning course of action, removing as it does one of the most powerful incentives there are to creative activity, namely, the disagreeable necessity of earning a living. Many artists, and by no means always the least gifted—rather the opposite—are notoriously indolent and unable to work save under the pressure of stern necessity. Our own Dr. Johnson, it may be remembered, on receiving a similar pension from the government of his day, practically ceased to do anything at all for the rest of his life except talk. That it should thus have led indirectly to Boswell's *Life* was a fortunate coincidence which can hardly be expected to occur again.

While as a general rule, then, the practical wisdom of thus generously subsidizing the artist seems very doubtful, the consequences in the particular case in question more than justified the action of the Finnish government. So far from impairing the composer's creative urge it seems rather to have stimulated it, and the vastness of Sibelius's output—greater, perhaps, than that of any other living composer—is undoubtedly due in part at least to the fact that he has been able to give his entire time and energy to the writing of music instead of having to teach or play some instrument in public for a living, or to engage in even less productive occupations, as most of his less fortunate colleagues are compelled to do.

It is true that Sibelius has done a certain amount of conducting in public, but only of his own works. About the time of his return to Finland his lifelong friend Robert Kajanus was, and still is, in command of the national orchestra in Helsingfors, and frequently gave the young composer opportunities for learning to conduct. In 1900, moreover, on the occasion of the great Paris Exhibition, the Finnish orchestra under Kajanus and Sibelius visited the French capital, giving concerts also in Stockholm, Göteborg, Malmö, Oslo, Copenhagen, Lübeck, Hamburg, Berlin, Amsterdam, Rotterdam, The Hague, and Brussels. On this extended tour Sibelius directed performances of several of his earlier orchestral compositions, and since that date he has visited practically every country in Europe, and also the United States, in order to conduct his works. England he has visited on several occasions, at first generally on the invitation and initiative of Sir Granville Bantock, one of his oldest friends and warmest admirers, and more recently, as in 1912 and 1921, on that of Sir Henry J. Wood, to whom, incidentally, one cannot be sufficiently grateful for the frequent opportunities he has afforded us of becoming acquainted with the music of Sibelius. Indeed, were it not for him it is exceedingly doubtful whether we should ever have heard any of the more important works, particularly the symphonies, until quite lately.

Many of Sibelius's works, especially during his middle period, were written abroad, in Germany, France, and Italy, where he has travelled frequently and extensively. Of late years, however, he has tended to spend less and less time in foreign lands, and now lives for the most part in almost monastic seclusion in his villa at Järvenpää, about twenty miles from Helsingfors, which he seldom leaves except to pay short visits to the capital.

During the Russian Revolution and its aftermath Sibelius, in common with most of his countrymen, underwent terrible experiences of which he prefers not to speak, and on which I consequently forbear to dwell. For the rest his later life has been the outwardly uneventful one of most creative artists, its most important landmarks being merely opus numbers.

The position which Sibelius occupies in the public life of his country is in many respects a unique one, and can only be compared with that enjoyed by d'Annunzio in Italy. He has probably done more to establish her position in the eyes of the world than all the rest of her inhabitants put together, and, to do her justice, she has always recognized this. Finland has for once triumphantly succeeded in disproving the time-honoured adage to the effect that a prophet is without honour in his own land. Sibelius is virtually the uncrowned king of Finland, a living symbol of her culture and political independence, and his fiftieth and sixtieth birthdays were celebrated as events of national importance. In return Sibelius has always been ready and willing to devote his art to the honour and service of his country, and a considerable number of his works have been written for special state occasions. This ideal relationship between an artist and his people is one that does great credit to both, and must excite the envy and admiration of those who have had the misfortune to be born in such barbarous and unenlightened lands as ours, where an artist is, to the ordinary man in the street, an object of derision and contempt.

Of the man himself, apart from his music, I am hardly qualified to write, seeing that my acquaintanceship with him is unfortunately of the slightest and most superficial order. In any case I must confess to a deeply rooted aversion, whole-heartedly shared by my subject, to the vulgar and impertinent curiosity which the modern public displays with regard to the private life of eminent persons. Consequently, even if I were in a position to gratify it, which I am not, I should nevertheless resolutely refrain from doing so. On the other hand, I do not agree with the purists who assert that a knowledge of an artist's personality is completely negligible and valueless in helping us to understand his work. With some artists, possibly it is so. It is unlikely, for example, that any addition to the sum of our knowledge concerning Bach, however substantial, would help us to understand or appreciate his work any better than we do now; with Mozart it is probably true to say that the more we learn about him the less we understand his art, the more enigmatic it becomes. But these are both exceptional cases; in general it may be said that a certain degree of knowledge concerning an artist's personality is often of considerable aid in elucidating his work. Sometimes a characteristic trait or chance observation, unimportant in itself, may afford a valuable clue to some aspect or other of a man's art. I know that I have often found it so myself; I have certainly found it so in the present instance. In the same way, in fact, that even a rudimentary and extremely superficial acquaintance with Finland and its culture has helped me now and then to understand certain things about his work, so my brief personal contact with the composer has similarly been of considerable assistance in shedding light upon certain of its features. It is only natural to suppose, therefore, that the reader will similarly benefit from being given a slight impression of Sibelius's personality, without it being necessary to intrude in unmannerly fashion upon his private life.

The typical Finn has been described by ethnologists as 'of middle height, muscular, broad-shouldered, with round head, broad face, concave nose, fair complexion, and blue or grey eyes'. This might almost be the passport description of Sibelius, so closely does he conform in physique to the national type. On the other hand, in temperament the Finn is reputed to be of a somewhat forbidding and inaccessible disposition, and no more inapt and inaccurate description of Sibelius in this respect could possibly be imagined. Courteous, affable, hospitable almost to excess, a true *grand seigneur*, one could not wish for a more pleasant companion or a more perfect host, and the times I have spent in his company, at Helsingfors and Järvenpää, will always be in retrospect amongst the most agreeable and memorable of my life.

This aspect of his personality probably represents the Swedish element in him, both of race and culture, for the Swedes are justly famed among peoples of the north for their possession to an unusual degree of the amiable social attributes above mentioned. With Sibelius, however, one very soon becomes aware of another side to his personality, deeper and more fundamental, a substratum of Finnish granite, as it were, underlying the polished and elegant Swedish surface. He unites in himself, in fact, the characteristic qualities of the two racial types; the traditional charm, affability, and *bonhomie* of the Swede, and the fiercely independent spirit, the sturdy self-reliance, the love of isolation and solitude, the extreme reserve, of the Finn. In the luxurious hotels and restaurants of Helsingfors he is the man of the world, an epicure with a refined and highly developed sense for all the graces and amenities of civilized life; in the austere and primitive surroundings of Järvenpää he is the mystic, the anchorite, the aloof and solitary dreamer. This duality of temperament, as we shall have occasion to remark later, is as striking a feature of the creative artist as of the man.

Sibelius will freely discuss any and every subject under the sun save only one, himself. Any attempt to discover what artistic projects he is engaged upon, what his methods of composition are, and so forth, invariably meet with an impenetrable barrier of reserve which one can only whole-heartedly respect. All I have been able to elicit from him on the latter point is the highly significant statement that for him orchestration as a thing in itself does not exist; the idea that a musical thought might occur to him in the abstract for which he had then to seek a suitable orchestration, or, conversely, that he might conceive a colour-scheme and then seek for musical material in which to embody it—both are alike unthinkable to him in connexion with his own work. In other words, the melodic, harmonic, and rhythmic material of his compositions is intimately bound up, from the very outset, with the instrumental medium employed.

In striking contrast to his studied reticence concerning his own music, Sibelius is singularly communicative of his opinions with regard to that of other composers, past and present, and many of them will be found to afford useful clues to the understanding of his art. In the first place he is to-day an uncompromising champion of pure music as opposed to operatic and programme music. Wagner, in particular, means, and always has meant, precisely nothing to Sibelius; for him, indeed, the art of Wagner is simply not music at all. The only operatic music that he unreservedly admires and enjoys is that of the Italians—Rossini, Bellini, Donizetti, Puccini even to a certain extent, but above all Verdi, for whom he has always cherished a deep respect and veneration.

Otherwise for the most part his tastes are both catholic and orthodox. I suspect, however—though I may quite possibly be wrong here—that despite his immense admiration for Bach he has more personal sympathy with Palestrina, Victoria, and other sixteenth-century masters of the polyphonic style; that despite his profound love of Mozart, Beethoven, and particularly the Beethoven of the posthumous string quartets, is temperamentally the more congenial to him. Beethoven, I should say without hesitation, is for Sibelius the supreme master.

His opinions on modern music in general are characterized by remarkable shrewdness, breadth, and tolerance. Referring to recent developments he once observed to me, more or less in these words: 'When you have lived as long as I have, and have seen so many new movements come and go for over forty years, you will not attach overmuch importance to them as such, but will recognize nevertheless that in each of them there is an element of truth and justification; that each draws attention to and stresses, sometimes unduly perhaps, some valuable aspect of musical art, some vital principle which might otherwise have been forgotten. They have all their *raison d'être*, in fact. The music of Schönberg and his followers, for example, is not sympathetic to me personally, but I freely recognize that such high aims, such sincerity, and such incontestably great gifts can only result in gain, in some valuable addition to the sum of music.'

On the subject of Stravinsky and his frequent and violent changes of style he was very non-committal, contenting himself with the observation that, although Beethoven managed to express the whole gamut of human and artistic experience in three styles, it was possible that Stravinsky needed six. One is irresistibly reminded of Clemenceau's famous epigram concerning President Wilson's Fourteen Points: 'le bon Dieu himself had only ten.' I am inclined to think that the fundamental implications of both remarks are much the same.

It only remains to be said, in conclusion, that the impression his personality makes upon one serves to confirm, and also to supplement in several important particulars, that made by his works, the dominating characteristic of both being a quite astonishing power, vigour, and overflowing vitality, always combined, however, with balance, serenity, and poise. The former qualities he doubtless owes to his Northern provenance, the latter to his deep humanistic culture, derived from his lifelong passion for the Greek and Latin classics. In this union of contrary qualities, generally, but wrongly, conceived as irreconcilable, lies the strength and greatness of Sibelius, both the man and the artist.

PART TWO

THE MUSIC

I. ORCHESTRAL AND CHORAL WORKS

THERE are two principal methods of making a critical survey of a composer's works; either one may deal with them in the order and succession in which they were written, or one can split them up into distinct formal categories or separate compartments, such as 'symphonies', 'chamber music', 'vocal works', and so forth. Both methods have their advantages and defects, and the one is better suited to some composers and the other to others. The former is the better to follow when concerned with one whose works, whatever their forms or *media*, reveal a definite stylistic progression from one to the other, or constitute successive stages or links in a single, unified line of thought; the latter is better suited to one whose style and mentality remain fundamentally unaltered throughout his career, the nature of each work being primarily determined by the form or medium employed. The first, generally speaking, is the method adopted with the romantic or innovating artist, the second with the classic or traditional. Schönberg, with whom each successive work is only a stepping-stone to the next, in the quest of some kind of musical philosophers' stone, is probably the best example of the former type; Brahms, who seems hardly to have altered in manner or developed mentally from his twenty-fifth year or so onwards, is a good instance of the latter.

Sibelius is a composer who does not belong wholly to either category but partakes to a certain extent of both. The writer of the article which deals with his work in Grove's *Dictionary of Music and Musicians* says that 'there is little change of outlook or steady progress to be discerned in his chronological catalogue', and in a sense this is correct. It is true, for example, that, as he says, 'the latest piano pieces are no better than, and not essentially different from, the first six Impromptus', and the same might be said of certain other aspects of his work, chiefly the less important ones. To say, however, that 'the early "En Saga" seems as mature and complete to-day as the last two symphonies' is a definitely misleading half-truth. Mature and complete 'En Saga' certainly is, but only in the same way that, for instance, Beethoven's piano sonata op. 31, no. 2, in D minor is mature and complete. That is to say, while it could not possibly be improved upon in any sense, and though it certainly is, in its way, a perfect masterpiece, it is none the less true that there is as great a gulf between it and the two latest symphonies as there is between the sonata of Beethoven referred to and the posthumous quartets. They belong to entirely different worlds, in fact, and between them there stretches a long, continuous, and complicated process of spiritual growth and stylistic development which is liable to be obscured if his work is divided up into formal categories, and can only be clearly brought out if it is considered in chronological sequence. On the other hand, his music is of such exceptional diversity and so often intimately conditioned by the specific nature of the form or medium that to pass, say, from a symphony to a group of songs, then to incidental music for a play, then to a set of piano pieces and so on, simply because they happen to have been written in that order, would obscure the issue just as effectually as would a rigorous adherence to the categorical method of treatment.

In order, therefore, to bring out clearly the inner logic and underlying significance of Sibelius's course of development, it will be necessary to resort to a compromise between the two procedures normally adopted, and, while preserving a chronological sequence in broad outline, to pass freely backwards and forwards when occasion demands in order that works belonging to the same or to a

F

similar category can be considered in relation to each other so far as is possible without breaking the continuity of the development as a whole. The symphonies in particular constitute a group of works so autonomous and self-contained, that they can be studied together in a chapter to themselves more conveniently and profitably than if they were dispersed singly here and there throughout our survey in strict accordance with the times at which they happen to have been written.

The early work of Sibelius, right up to his twenty-fifth year, consists almost exclusively of chamber music, written, moreover, in the strictest classical form and style. It is chiefly interesting for the way in which, side by side with compositions which are little if anything more than promising student exercises, one occasionally comes across an example which reveals the presence of a considerable degree of genuine creative ability. At the same time it must be confessed that even the best of them—such as the accomplished string quartet in B flat, the only one to which the composer has accorded the dignity of an opus number—are singularly lacking in individuality, and indeed in all the qualities which one finds in his mature works. Whether good, bad, or indifferent, in fact, they are all somewhat impersonal. Indeed, the qualities which they display are in many respects the very opposite to those which were shortly after to be unfolded in the huge symphony for soloists, chorus, and orchestra entitled 'Kullervo', in which Sibelius finds himself for the first time. In this respect, it may be observed, there is a striking parallel between his development and that of Richard Strauss, his contemporary and senior by only a year, who similarly produced a large quantity of extremely competent but quite undistinguished student work before suddenly finding himself in works on a large scale such as 'Macbeth' and 'Don Juan'.

Kullervo, as we have already observed (p. 33), is one of the chief characters in the *Kalevala*—a strange figure, whose whole life, from birth to death, is one long tale of tragedy unrelieved by any glimmering of light or consolation. The score of the work is of epic proportions, running to no less than 448 pages and consisting of five movements: (I) 'Introduction', (II) 'Kullervo's Youth', (III) 'Kullervo and his Sister', (IV) 'Kullervo goes forth to Battle', and (V) 'The Death of Kullervo'. The voices take part in the third and fifth movements only, the others being purely instrumental.

After the 'Introduction' in which the tragic key-note of the whole work is sounded and the chief thematic material presented, there follows a sombre and passionate movement in which the misery and hardships of the hero's early years are depicted. The third movement recounts the story of how Kullervo, travelling homewards one day in his sleigh, woos successively but in vain two maidens, and finally wins a third to his desire by means of gifts and cajolery, only to discover after it was too late that she was his sister from whom he had been parted since infancy. Stricken by remorse for their involuntary crime, the maiden throws herself into a neighbouring torrent and is drowned. An orchestral interlude follows, depicting Kullervo's vain attempt to find oblivion in warlike activities, and the last movement relates how, with his faithful dog at his side, he took his way through the forest until he came to the spot where the fatal meeting with his sister had taken place, and there, drawing his sword,

> On the ground the haft set firmly,
> On the heath the hilt pressed tightly;
> Turned the point against his bosom,
> And upon the point he threw him,
> Thus he found the death he sought for,
> Cast himself into destruction.

Even so the young man perished,
Thus died Kullervo the hero,
Thus the hero's life was ended,
Perished thus the hapless hero.

The work remains unpublished, and the manuscript full score is preserved in the library of the University at Helsingfors, where I have been able to study it. Without pretending to a sufficient degree of acquaintance with the work to be able to criticize it in detail, such brief and cursory examination of it as I was able to make was nevertheless enough to give me a very high opinion of its merits. 'Kullervo', indeed, is a work of great strength and marked individuality, and one can only express surprise at the fact that it has been allowed to remain in manuscript.

For this, however, the composer himself is at least partly responsible. He confesses to being not entirely satisfied with the work as it stands, and while admitting that he might conceivably be able to remedy the more outstanding defects by rewriting it here and there, he is nevertheless disinclined to do so, being of the opinion that the faults and imperfections of a work are often so intimately bound up with its very nature, that an attempt to rectify them without impairing it as a whole must almost inevitably fail. It is certainly true that the retouching of isolated parts of a work is apt to be unsatisfactory, in evidence of which one need look no farther than the flagrant example of the new Venusberg music which Wagner wrote for the Paris production of 'Tannhäuser' in 1861, which is on such a very much higher musical level than anything else in the work that when it is substituted for the original version the effect of the whole is utterly destroyed. The only really satisfactory method of re-writing a work is to recast it from beginning to end, and Sibelius no doubt feels that he is more profitably engaged in writing new works than in re-writing old ones. In this he is probably correct. In any case the artist who spends his time revising his early productions is seldom of the first rank. It is generally symptomatic of a lack of creative power.

The chances are, then, that 'Kullervo' will never see the light of day, which is greatly to be regretted seeing that much of the music, particularly that of the third movement, is as fine as anything Sibelius has written during his early period.

'Kullervo' is not only a landmark in the composer's career but also in the musical history of his country. Hitherto her most eminent composers had been foreigners—such as Pacius, a German—or, when Finnish by birth, predominantly Swedish in feeling and inclination. 'Kullervo' was the first large-scale piece of music, based upon a national subject and set to words in the native language, which Finland could recognize as her own. With 'Kullervo', in fact, Finland became musically articulate; with Sibelius's next important work, the tone-poem 'En Saga', op. 9, for orchestra, she definitely entered the European musical concert and made her existence felt for the first time in the history of music.

'En Saga', indeed, is a work which can be placed alongside the musical products of any other country without having any need to fear from the comparison; it is the first work of its composer which one can unhesitatingly describe as a masterpiece. From the very opening bars with the mysterious, beckoning call of the horns, the bare open fifths of the tremolos and arpeggios of the muted strings, the strident dissonances of the wood-wind, right through to the catastrophic climax in the brass and the sombre, whispered close in the lower strings—the whole work is one of astonishing power and originality, quite unlike anything previously written by any other composer.

One of the chief attractions of 'En Saga' is the

quite exceptional wealth of melodic invention that
it reveals, at least three of the leading themes being
of such outstanding beauty and distinction that any
one of them alone would in itself be enough to
make the fortune of a work. A peculiar feature of
the texture is the unusually extensive employment
of pedal-points. For example, on the first appearance of the third principal theme one finds no fewer
than 82 consecutive bars of pedal for the double-
basses, to say nothing of various other internal
pedals at the same time, while a little farther on a
sequence of 28 bars of held notes for the horns is
followed without a break by one of 22 and another
of 79 on the double-basses, and after only a few
bars of respite by still another of 70. These are by
no means isolated examples; on the contrary, it is
no exaggeration to say that from beginning to end
there is literally hardly a bar in the work without
a pedal-point, with the exception of a passage for
strings alone of some twenty bars or so about half-
way through. It is this technical peculiarity that is
primarily responsible for the dark, threatening,
sombre tone-quality which gives such a distinctive
character to the music.

'En Saga' was the first work of Sibelius to make
his name known outside Finland. Introduced into

Germany by Busoni in the 'nineties it created a deep impression, and rapidly made its way to other countries, where it is still to-day the most widely known and frequently performed of all his more important works—the only one, indeed, that can be said to be at all familiar to concert audiences. As a natural result of the vogue and popularity of this one work and the comparative neglect of the rest, there is a tendency to regard the peculiar individual features and qualities of 'En Saga' as being characteristic of all the composer's music, and consequently to think of him as one exclusively preoccupied with the sombre and gloomy aspects of things. This is certainly the popular idea of Sibelius, and even for many musicians his name invariably connotes the aural equivalents of darkness, winter, storm, cold, night, and so forth. Nothing could be more mistaken. Sibelius has admittedly written gloomy and tragic works, but I very much doubt whether on the whole they form a perceptibly greater proportion of his output than of any other composer's, generally speaking. It is true that many of his most important and characteristic works are of this type, but it is certainly not true that all of them are. He may have explored the arctic regions of music more thoroughly than any other composer before him, but that has not prevented him from visiting more temperate and even tropic climes as well. And if 'Kullervo' and 'En Saga' represent what one might call the dark and wintry side of his art, one finds in the 'Vårsång' ('Spring Song') for orchestra, written about the same time, a music of quite different character.

The sub-title of the work, 'La Tristesse du Printemps', might perhaps seem to belie this to some extent. It has certainly led impressionable literary commentators to find in it an expression of sadness and regret at the shortness and evanescence of the northern springtide, and one even hears conductors trying vainly to extract tragedy and gloom from its suave and innocent concords, with comic results. At most it might be conceded that there is a strain of wistful and elegiac melancholy in the middle minor section, but for the rest the mood is tranquil and serene throughout. The sub-title, in fact, is self-evidently a mere afterthought of a subjective kind, and is in consequence somewhat misleading.

An interesting feature of the work, by the way, is the striking affinity that the long-drawn melody on which it is chiefly based bears to many of the spring songs and *reverdies* of ancient Provençal music, with their tendency to oscillate ambiguously between tonality and modality. Since it is highly improbable that Sibelius could have been acquainted with this old music, the decipherment and publication of which are of quite recent date, one can only attribute this remarkable resemblance to a kind of subtle correspondence between certain musical procedures and certain conceptions. That Sibelius, in fact, a modern Finn, should have arrived at virtually the same melodic formulas as those encountered in the music of the thirteenth-century troubadours and minstrels of Provence in giving expression to the same order of sensations and emotions, suggests the possibility that music is a much more exact language than aestheticians are willing to admit.

Even more strongly contrasted with the gloomy mood to which Sibelius is wrongly supposed to confine himself is the music of 'Karelia', op. 10 and 11, comprising an overture and a suite in three movements. The province of Karelia which gives its name to the music is the south-easternmost part of Finland, and its inhabitants have the reputation of being of a more vivacious and affable disposition than the rest of the Finnish race. Certainly nothing could be gayer, livelier, more spontaneous than this music, which is in the lightest and brightest tones throughout. It is interesting to note, moreover, that in writing music ostensibly Karelian in character and style Sibelius approaches as closely to that of Russia as Karelia itself does to Russian soil. The thematic material is sometimes strongly suggestive of various Slavonic masters, and the eightfold repetition of a single phrase in the trio of the 'Alla Marcia' in the suite is as characteristic of Russian music as it is rare in that of Finland. 'Karelia', indeed, is the sole work of Sibelius that one could easily believe to have been written by a Russian if one were to hear it without knowing who had composed it.

'Karelia' was originally planned as an accompaniment to a series of historical *tableaux* arranged by the students of Viborg University in 1893, depicting incidents in the ancient history and folk-life of the province. Sibelius composed a great deal of music for the occasion, but apart from what is contained in these two opus numbers it would seem to have disappeared or been destroyed. The 'Scènes Historiques', op. 25, and 'Finlandia', op. 26, came into being in the same way, in the form of incidental music to a series of *tableaux*, illustrating episodes taken from Finnish mythology and history from the earliest times up to the present day, which were

performed on some patriotic occasion at Helsingfors. Again, much of this music has disappeared;
'Finlandia', for example, is described as op. 26,
no. 7, but none of the remaining numbers seems to
have been published or even to have survived at all.

The 'Scènes Historiques' are not on the whole
among Sibelius's most interesting or significant productions, apart from the masterly orchestration
which is a constant factor in all his work, and this
also applies to the second series, op. 66, which
appeared much later though probably based to
some extent at least on the same material. They are
neither strongly personal nor, curiously enough,
strongly national, as one might have expected them
to be in view of the circumstances under which
they were written, but are rather lacking in definite
character of any kind. 'Finlandia' is in a different
category altogether; whether one likes it or not the
mere fact of its great popularity should not, I think,
be allowed to blind us to the fact that it is a work
of considerable originality and intrinsic merit. One's
only objection to it is that its immense and quite
disproportionate vogue has probably been to a great
extent the cause of the comparative neglect accorded
to his more important and significant works.
Sibelius for most people is, and always has been,

the composer of 'Finlandia' and 'Valse triste'; they do not wish to hear anything else.

While staying at Kuopio in the interior of Finland during the summer of 1893 Sibelius became acquainted with a writer named J. H. Erkko, who suggested that they should collaborate in an opera. It was to be called 'Weneen luominen', 'The Building of the Boat', and the underworld of Finnish mythology, Tuonela, was to be the scene of part of the action. Sibelius started work on the music, but after a time, finding the operatic medium uncongenial to him, he abandoned the idea, but not before he had written what was to have been the prelude to the opera, namely, the piece entitled 'The Swan of Tuonela', eventually published as the third number in a suite of four 'Legends' for orchestra, op. 22. The other three numbers, 'Lemminkäinen and the Maiden', 'Lemminkäinen in Tuonela', and 'The Return of Lemminkäinen', were not written till three years later, and of them only the last-named has been published. The other two remain in manuscript and appear to be in the possession of a Finnish society called *Kalevalaseura*. Something should be done about this if, as one has no reason to doubt, these movements are of similar calibre to that of the two published ones, which probably mark the highest point to which Sibelius attains in his early period.

The score of 'The Swan of Tuonela' bears the following inscription: 'Tuonela, the land of death, the hell of Finnish mythology, is surrounded by a large river with black waters and a rapid current, on which the Swan of Tuonela floats majestically, singing.' It is written for the unusual combination of cor anglais solo, one oboe, one bass clarinet, two bassoons, four horns, three trombones, harp, kettledrums, bass drum, and muted strings divided into an immense number of parts throughout save for a unisonal passage towards the close. It will be noted that all the bright-toned instruments, such as flutes, clarinets, and trumpets, are excluded from the scheme, the result being a prevailing tone-quality of an exceptionally dark and mysterious kind. Unusual effects of sonority, moreover, are attained by means of various special devices which occur in the course of the work—soft chords of a minor third for the kettledrums, *tremolo col legno* for the muted and divided strings, doubled by harmonics and other held notes, and so forth, anticipating in many directions the experimental orchestration of so much modern music.

The work is equally noteworthy in other

respects. The slow, gently swaying, hypnotic nine-four rhythm, the strange, poignant harmonies of the strings at the beginning and close, the long, winding, dream-like melody for the cor anglais which persists throughout almost without a break —a masterly piece of organic construction, by the way, consisting of some sixty bars which contain hardly any repetition save of one haunting, perpetually recurring phrase—these are all features of singular beauty and originality. Nowhere else has Sibelius more perfectly realized the strange, magical beauty that lies at the heart of Finnish mythology. The whole work, indeed, although it consists of no more than a hundred bars and is contained in fifteen pages of full score only, is one of the most deeply poetic and imaginative things in modern music.

It would be difficult to find a more complete and striking contrast than that between 'The Swan of Tuonela' and its companion piece 'The Return of Lemminkäinen'. The latter is scored for the ordinary full orchestra, the *tempo* is that of a terrific headlong *con fuoco* in two-four rhythm, and the thematic material consists of tiny scraps and fragments, tossed about from one group of instruments to another, which are gradually and progressively welded together into an organic whole as the work proceeds—a method of construction which, as we shall see, is peculiarly characteristic of Sibelius's later style and makes its appearance here for the first time.

The programmatic basis of the work is a passage in the 30th runo of the *Kalevala* which tells how the hero returns to his own country after his unsuccessful expedition against Pohjola, the Northland:

Then the lively Lemminkäinen
From his cares constructed horses,
Coursers black composed from trouble,
Reins from evil days he fashioned,
Saddles from his secret sorrows,
Then his horse's back he mounted,
On his white-front courser mounted,
And he rode upon his journey.

The most remarkable feature of the work, perhaps, is the degree of restraint and economy of instrumental means employed to produce an effect of tremendous tension and energy which never slackens for a single moment. The full forces of the orchestra are held in check throughout with an iron hand until the very end, when they are unleashed in a great triumphant fanfare of exceptional brilliance.

G

A later orchestral work based on the *Kalevala* is 'Pohjola's Daughter', a symphonic fantasia, op. 49. The poem attached to the score is a paraphrase of an episode which recounts how Väinämöinen, also on his way back from the Northland, comes suddenly upon the maiden of Pohjola, seated aloft upon a shining rainbow, spinning. Enchanted by her radiant beauty he beseeches her to come down to him and join him, which she refuses to do except on condition that he will, by means of his magic arts, make for her a boat out of the pieces of her spindle. Väinämöinen toils in vain, unable to discover the correct magical formula, until finally in despair he relinquishes his attempt and, leaping back into his sleigh, continues his homeward journey.

'Pohjola's Daughter' belongs more definitely to the category of 'programme' music than any of Sibelius's other works. In order to understand and appreciate 'En Saga', 'Lemminkäinen', or 'The Swan of Tuonela', nothing more is strictly needed than the titles, if even those, but here the musical development is to some extent conditioned by the poem. For example, the semiquaver figure met with at the outset, which constitutes the *leitmotiv* of the whole work, is clearly descriptive of the motion of the spinning wheel, and various other passages can be definitely identified with literary or pictorial suggestions in the programme, such as the appearance of the maiden on the rainbow and her mockery of the hero. At the same time the music is not unintelligible apart from the programme, as is that of so many symphonic poems.

'Pohjola's Daughter' is scored for an unusually large orchestra, including, in addition to the ordinary forces, piccolo, cor anglais, bass clarinet, double-bassoon, two cornets, and harp. As this would suggest, the chief interest of the work is colouristic. From the dark, sombre harmonies of the opening to the brilliant, glittering texture of the 'rainbow' music, the whole gamut of the tonal spectrum is traversed from end to end. This work, in fact, probably represents the farthest point to which Sibelius attains in respect of sumptuousness of colour and elaboration of texture. Thenceforward one notes a constantly growing tendency in the direction of economy of orchestral means and simplicity of style.

In addition to these purely orchestral works inspired by the *Kalevala* Sibelius has also made several vocal settings of parts of the actual text in addition to the early 'Kullervo' which we have already noticed. Of these one of the most important is 'The Origin of Fire' ('Ukko the Firemaker'), op. 32, for baritone solo, male voice chorus, and orchestra, written on the occasion of the inauguration of the Finnish National Theatre at Helsingfors in 1902. The words, which are taken from the 47th runo, describe how Ukko, the Zeus of Finnish mythology—the God on High, the Great Lord of the Air, the Mighty Father of the Sky, the Ruler of Thunderclouds, as he is variously called—restores to mankind the light and sunshine of which they had been robbed by Louhi, the 'old and gap-toothed dame of Pohja', the arch-villainess of the *Kalevala*.

The opening baritone solo depicts the state of utter darkness and desolation in which the whole world lies plunged, and Ukko's vain search throughout the universe for the missing sun and moon. The chorus then enters and relates how the god struck a spark from his gleaming sword-blade and gave it to the Maiden of the Air to nurse and tend.

> And the foolish maiden dropped it,
> From her hands the fire dropped downward,
> From the fingers of its guardian.
> Then the sky was cleft asunder,
> All the air was filled with windows,

Burst asunder by the fire-sparks,
As the red drop quick descended,
And a gap gleamed forth in heaven,
As it through the clouds dropped downward,
Through nine heavens the drop descended,
Through six spangled vaults of heaven.

'The Origin of Fire' is a work of epic power and
grandeur, masterly in its gradual emergence from
the atmosphere of darkness and gloom of the opening baritone solo, into the radiance and glow of the
final choral section. That such an admirable work
should be completely unknown and neglected is
all the more inexcusable in that it has been provided
with both German and English translations, but I
doubt whether it has ever been performed in either
country.

Even finer, however, and consequently even more
completely unknown and neglected, if possible, is
'Luonnotar', op. 70, for soprano solo and orchestra,
a setting of words from the first runo, narrating the
Finnish legend of the Creation, and the birth of the
hero Väinämöinen from the union of the winds and
waves with Luonnotar, the Virgin of the Air. This
work represents one of the highest pinnacles in the
whole range of Sibelius's creations, and consequently
in the entire range of modern music; yet it is not

merely unsung, unplayed, unread, but its very publishers seem to be unaware of its existence, seeing that a request for a copy was met by a polite expression of regret that no such title was to be found in their catalogue. It is true that the full score is still unpublished, but that only makes it worse, since the orchestration is of surpassing interest, even for Sibelius. It is, indeed, one of the most remarkable scores of modern times, abounding in curious and interesting experiments in sonority. A particularly noteworthy feature is the writing for the kettledrums, six in number and requiring two players, which are continually playing in minor seconds simultaneously. Striking, too, is the writing for double-basses, and at the opposite extreme for the piccolos playing open fifths low down in their compass or doubling the clarinets at three and the bass clarinet at four octaves' distance. Particularly arresting, however, are the last pages with the semitonal clashes for drums, a four-part double-bass *divisi*, dissonant polytonal harmonies for strings and harps, and over it all an exquisitely poignant melodic line for the voice, rising and falling like the flight of a wounded bird.

With all its bold experiments, however, which are sometimes exceedingly difficult to realize in the mind's ear, so to speak, one feels a certainty of touch and an inevitability which are often lacking in the similar procedures of most other modern composers. In all the works of Sibelius one has heard it is difficult to think of a single miscalculated effect of orchestration; it is consequently only reasonable to assume that his instinct is as sure here as it is everywhere else in one's experience, in spite of the undoubted strangeness of much of the music on paper. His experiments, moreover, are never indulged in for their own sakes, as ends in themselves, but are always kept strictly subservient to his expressive intentions.

'The Song of Väino' for chorus and orchestra, op. 110, one of Sibelius's most recent compositions, is a work which lends partial support to the view already quoted to the effect that no consistent line of development is to be discerned in his chronological catalogue. It is a setting of the concluding section of the 43rd runo of the *Kalevala*, and consists chiefly in an invocation addressed to the creator, Jumala, by Väinämöinen, imploring favours and protection. The music is broad, simple, and dignified both in conception and style, but lacking in the inspiration and the transfiguring imaginative power of his best work. Without the evidence of its opus number one would have assumed it to be an early composition.

'Tapiola', on the other hand, a tone-poem for large orchestra, op. 112, written in the very same year, is in many respects the culminating point of his entire creative activity, and a consummate masterpiece which could only be the outcome of a long process of spiritual growth and development. It is music of the most extraordinary simplicity and directness, yet there is not one bar in it, from first to last, that could possibly have been written by any other composer.

The work takes its name from Tapio, the forest god of Finnish mythology—the Old Man of the Woods, the Elder of the Hills, the Master of the Wasteland—and the motto prefixed to the score is as follows:

Widespread they stand, the Northland's dusky forests,
Ancient, mysterious, brooding savage dreams,
Within them dwells the Forest's mighty God
And woodsprites in the gloom weave magic secrets.

It begins with a phrase given out by the strings which consists of two bars of a few notes only, moving in conjunct motion within the compass of a fourth—as plain, as simple, as straightforward outwardly, as a fragment of Gregorian chant, yet so pregnant with possibilities that it is no exaggeration to say that the entire work evolves from it. At the very outset it is repeated with variations by different instrumental combinations no fewer than twenty-two times, and the transformations it subsequently undergoes are infinite in number and extent. Even when the theme itself is not actually there in some form or another, which is seldom, it makes its spiritual presence felt throughout. The denouement of the work is reached with a rising *crescendo* passage of chromatics for the strings alone, extending over thirty-seven bars, which attains to an unimaginable pitch of intensity, and culminates in a truly terrific and overwhelming outburst from the whole orchestra—one of the greatest climaxes in all music, like a convulsion of nature, or the unchaining of some elemental force.

No mere words can hope to convey one tithe of the grandeur and sublimity, the sheer originality and imaginative power, which inform the whole work both in broadest outline and in the minutest details of the scoring. Even if Sibelius had written nothing else this one work would be sufficient to entitle him to a place among the greatest masters of all time.

II. MISCELLANEOUS COMPOSITIONS

IN the foregoing chapter we have been almost exclusively concerned with those works of Sibelius which, in the restricted sense already defined and laid down earlier in the book, may be described as national; that is to say, those works which are based upon a Finnish text or subject, or which reflect in some way or other the characteristics of the country or the people. In the present chapter I propose to deal mainly with what may be called the eclectic or cosmopolitan side of his art.

The distinction is in certain respects a real one, in others somewhat artificial and merely employed for the sake of convenience. Some of his works belong definitely to the one category, some to the other, while some again stand so near either side of the dividing line that it is a matter of indifference to which of the two one assigns them. Again, this hard-and-fast distinction fails to discriminate between works which are settings of Finnish subjects or texts, but of which the music is in no way recognizably national, and works which are either based upon alien texts or subjects, but in which definite traces of a Finnish musical accent can be discerned. On the whole, however, it is I think true to say that the broad division into national and eclectic, Finnish and cosmopolitan, corresponds to a real psychological duality.

In dealing with this second category it will be convenient to turn our attention first to those works which are associated with foreign literary or dramatic conceptions, and then to works of a purely musical order. And since Sweden is the country most closely connected with Finland, both geographically and culturally, we shall begin to follow the composer's spiritual Odyssey there, with a series of works for chorus and orchestra, written to Swedish texts in 1898–1900, and rather curiously entitled 'Improvisations'.

Of these the last only, 'Snöfrid', op. 29, a setting of a poem of Rydberg, has so far been published. It is certainly by a long way the best of them. The form is unusual: a series of short movements, linked together by transition passages, which are quite distinct from each other in key, *tempo*, and thematic content, followed by a passage of orchestrally accompanied recitation, and concluding with a kind of long choral epilogue gradually winding its way to an exultant close. Musically it is a work of high merit; the other two, 'Sandels' (to words by

Runeberg), op. 28, and 'Islossningen' (to words of Topelius), op. 30, are of less intrinsic distinction and are chiefly interesting as experiments in the direction of a somewhat novel form, consisting in the application to choral writing of the methods employed in solo dramatic recitative or narrative declamation. They are, in fact, intensifications of poetry rather than works of inherent musical significance. The words are of greater moment than the music, consequently contrapuntal devices which tend to impede their natural flow and movement are wholly avoided, and the choral writing is frequently in unisons and octaves, with the orchestra providing a tonal background or accompaniment of no great independent interest. They should prove highly effective in performance, none the less.

In view of the essentially dramatic character of these works it is somewhat surprising that Sibelius should always have evinced such a marked aversion to the operatic form. We have seen how his first dramatic project was speedily abandoned, and the fact that he did subsequently write an opera, 'The Maid in the Tower' (1896), is explained solely by his acceptance of a definite commission to do so, and not by any inner prompting or inclination on his part. The composer himself regards it as completely negligible, and a superficial scrutiny of the rather illegible manuscript piano score, which is all I have been able to see, tended to confirm his own unfavourable judgement.

This distaste and comparative incapacity for writing operatic music is all the more curious and inexplicable in view of the vast quantity of incidental music he has composed for plays, which is frequently not only of a high order of musical interest but often exceedingly apt dramatically also. The explanation of its existence is to be found in the great demand which prevails in northern countries for plays provided with musical interludes and accompaniments, of which Grieg's 'Peer Gynt' is the most familiar example; and this demand is in its turn explained by the fact that in many of the large cities the opera and the drama are housed in the same building, and plays and operas alternate with each other on different nights—the consequence being that the playwright and theatrical producer have at their disposal a large orchestra which would otherwise be lying idle. That Sibelius should have been frequently approached with suggestions that he should contribute incidental music of this kind is not surprising; what is surprising is, firstly, that he should so often have complied with them, in view of his aversion to the theatre, and secondly, that the result should have been so frequently admirable.

The explanation, I think, is to be found in the fact that in this branch of his activities Sibelius resembles those artists of the Middle Ages and the Renaissance who accepted as a matter of course and without questioning every kind of commission that was offered to them. Was it an altar-piece for the neighbouring church, a series of frescoes illustrating the life of some saint for the local convent, an easel portrait of the reigning prince? They could always be relied upon to provide exactly what was wanted, and at the same time to carry out their task with a never-failing fund of invention and an assured technical mastery.

So with Sibelius here. In the many works of this kind that he has produced he is not the creative artist occupied in expressing his innermost thoughts and feelings, but the skilled craftsman who has been called in to execute a certain task in accordance with certain definite conditions. But while it is true that it is all 'occasional' music, written to order, it is never merely perfunctory, even when one feels that the undertaking has not been particularly congenial to him personally. There may often be little, and

94

sometimes nothing, in it of Sibelius himself, nothing that would have got itself written had he not been commissioned to do it, but the pure craftsman's interest in a piece of work to be done, and the high level of technical accomplishment invariably attained, often give his work in this category an intrinsic interest which, if not of the highest order, is nevertheless by no means negligible and frequently considerable. Much of it, too, retains a permanent value apart from the original purpose for which it was designed. The 'King Christian II' of Adolf Paul, for example, is a play unknown outside Scandinavia, and more or less forgotten inside, but the music Sibelius wrote for its production in 1898 is still to be heard in the concert-room.

The play deals with the story of the love of Christian II, king of Denmark, Norway, and Sweden, for a Dutch girl of common origin named Dyveke, and its tragic sequel in her assassination. Sibelius's music—or at any rate all of it that has been published—consists of seven pieces; a simple and moving elegy for strings only (played behind the curtain as a prelude), a charming miniature musette for two clarinets and two bassoons, a minuet for flutes, clarinets, and strings, a 'Fool's Song' with accompaniment of strings and harp in which the spirit of northern folk-song and balladry is admirably seized, and three pieces of larger and more elaborate design for full orchestra—Nocturne, Serenade, and Ballad—of which the latter is the most important: a wild and stormy movement in which the tragic denouement of the drama receives musical embodiment. Without any self-conscious attempt at archaism the music throughout gives a vivid picture of Swedish life at the time of the Renaissance.

Another Swedish play, but of a very different kind, to which Sibelius has contributed incidental music is 'Svanehvit' ('Swanwhite') of August Strindberg. The author, in a note to the play, says: 'I had long had it in mind to skim the cream off our most beautiful folk-ballads and to make them into a picture for the stage. Then Maeterlinck came across my path, and under the influence of his puppet plays, which are not meant for the regular stage, I wrote "Swanwhite".' Nothing could be more remote from the ordinary conception of Strindberg as a morbid and gloomy maniac than the aspect of him presented by this charming fairy story, and just as the play reveals an unsuspected side to the dramatist so does the graceful and delicately tinted music that Sibelius has provided for it show the composer in a comparatively unfamiliar but equally sympathetic light.

The score consists of seven pieces for various small orchestral combinations. Particularly attractive numbers are 'The Peacock', with its upper pedal for oboes and clarinets sustained throughout; 'The Harp', an exquisitely poetic little fantasy; 'Listen, the Robin sings', an imaginative piece of tone-painting in miniature; and 'The Maiden with the Roses', a charming little lyric.

The music to 'Scaramouche', a tragic pantomime by Poul Knudsen, is also in fantastic vein. The scenario, based upon the hackneyed theme of the sinister stranger who lures away a wife from her husband, is unfortunately weak. In consequence, probably, the composer does not seem to be interested in his task as he certainly seems to be in 'Swanwhite'. With all its technical brilliance and mastery one feels something rather mechanical and uninspired about it.

The incidental music to Maeterlinck's 'Pelléas et Mélisande', on the other hand, if hardly one of his most personal productions, is something more than mere craftsmanship. Curiously enough, this music written to a play by a Flemish dramatist is more definitely Finnish in feeling than much that Sibelius

H

97

has composed to national subjects. It was no mere caprice or extraneous form of inducement that can have led him to incorporate the greater part of it, transcribed for the piano, in the volume of selected pieces entitled 'Sibeliana: Scenes from the Land of a Thousand Lakes', in which, for example, the piece originally called 'Mélisande' becomes 'Evening by the Woodland Lake', and 'The Death of Mélisande' becomes 'The Sun Sinks'. The latter titles, indeed, strike one as being much more in keeping with the character of the music than the original ones. However that may be, several of the numbers are amongst Sibelius's finest work in miniature forms. They are scored for a small orchestra consisting of flute, oboe (cor anglais), two clarinets, two bassoons, two horns, kettledrums, and the usual strings.

The music to 'Belshazzar's Feast' by Hjalmar Procopé is in striking contrast to the unconscious, involuntary nationalism of 'Pelléas', and is the only work of Sibelius in which one finds a deliberate cultivation of exotic local colour. It is written for an orchestra of two flutes, oboe, two clarinets, two horns, strings, and a battery of percussion instruments, and is in the familiar pseudo-eastern tradition. The titles of two of the numbers, 'Oriental Procession' and 'Khadra's Dance', sufficiently indicate their character—the first beginning *pianissimo*, rising to *fortissimo*, and dying away again, with *ostinato* figures and pedals throughout and oriental melismata for the wood-wind; the second, another 'Anitra's Dance'. It could all have been done by any one else, though probably not so well.

The incidental music to the 'Jedermann' of Hugo von Hoffmannsthal is another example of Sibelius's phenomenal versatility. It is far more of an integral part of the drama than usual, and consists mainly of small pieces which are of little value apart from their dramatic context. One or two of the longer numbers, however, are of quite exceptional interest, and far transcend the category of mere conscientious craftsmanship. Particularly fine is the music accompanying the dialogue between Jedermann and Werke for muted strings *divisi*, with the parts all moving semitonally for over eighty bars before the interval of a whole tone, even, is sounded. Gradually and almost imperceptibly a deeply expressive theme for second violins emerges from this chromatic chiaroscuro, and a definite tonality makes itself felt. The conception is simple, obvious even, but the workmanship is exceedingly subtle and ingenious. Very striking, too, in their different ways are the last two numbers—the long-drawn-out discords of the one, the bitonal harmonies of the other, and in both the skill with which the music remains a background to the spoken word without losing intrinsic interest.

But Sibelius's highest achievement up to the present in the department of incidental music is his last—that which he wrote for the production of Shakespeare's 'The Tempest' at the Royal Theatre in Copenhagen in 1926, comprising in its published form a prelude and two extensive orchestral suites in seventeen movements for large orchestra. I would go even farther and say that it is in my opinion the greatest incidental music of modern times, and is only equalled in older times by that of Purcell. Several fortunate circumstances have contributed to this: firstly, the composer's deep love of Shakespeare in general and of this play in particular; secondly, the fact that 'The Tempest' lends itself freely to musical elaboration and, indeed, imperiously demands it—in witness whereof one need only point to the large number of places in the stage directions in which the aid of music is definitely invoked by the dramatist; thirdly, the immense resources placed at the composer's disposal by the peculiar conditions of the Scandinavian theatre to which allusion has already been made. Where else, indeed, except perhaps at festival performances in such places as Salzburg, is there a theatre willing to provide, or even able to accommodate, such a large orchestra as that employed by Sibelius here, including in addition to the ordinary large orchestra two piccolos, a clarinet in E flat, bass clarinet, harp, and a large assortment of percussion instruments? If only for this reason, it is sad to reflect, this magnificent musical transfiguration of Shakespeare's masterpiece is unlikely ever to be heard in his own country under the conditions for which it was written. Even in the concert-room, however, much, if not most, of the music has sufficient independent interest of its own to justify its separate performance. Some of it, indeed, is among the finest music of his later period. The Prelude, for example, is one of the grandest pieces of storm music in existence. One might legitimately have doubted whether it was any longer possible in these days to extract another ounce of musical substance from the hackneyed formulas which a piece in this *genre* must inevitably employ, yet Sibelius succeeds in doing so, and more. All the old familiar ingredients—chromatic scales for the strings, whole-tone harmonies for the wind, the employment of a vast battery of percussion instruments, the confused rumblings of the double-basses

—they are all there, but they are exploited with such technical resource and infused with such an intensity of inspiration that they take on a new lease of life.

Other notable pieces in this 'Tempest' music are the first movement of the first suite, with its strange, angular flute melody over an accompaniment of muted strings and a mysterious pedal note for basses and bass clarinet which continually recurs unaltered whatever the key; and the piece entitled 'Caliban'—inhuman, baleful, demoniac—with its elaborate use of percussion including kettledrums, bass and side drums, cymbals, xylophone, triangle. In the one Sibelius distils a remote, magical beauty from what are technically extreme discords; in the other he conveys an impression of horror and repulsiveness without employing any discords at all—as every other composer would have done— but by merely distorting ordinary consonances, and placing them in false relations to each other. This is in its way a sheer masterstroke of psychological characterization which tells us more about Caliban than any number of volumes of critical analysis and exegesis.

In such things as this—for there are many other equally happy strokes of this kind in the work—

one feels the presence of a born musical dramatist, and one can only regret that the composer has not made a full-fledged opera out of it. It is at least certain that no other composer before him has so well realized in music the fantastic, haunting, magical quality of 'The Tempest'.

To the category of incidental music belongs also the contribution made by Sibelius to the play written by his brother-in-law, Eero Järnefelt, entitled 'Kuolema', of which the all too familiar 'Valse triste' forms a part—a little work which has done more to make his name known to the many and to injure his reputation in the eyes of the few than everything else he has written, put together. It is exceedingly difficult to see why it should have done either. If one tries to look at it in absolute critical detachment—admittedly a difficult thing to do—it does not appear to merit either its immense vogue or the frenzy of indignation into which it throws so many good people, but to be merely an original, ingenious, and highly effective essay in the musical *macabre*, and nothing more. It is of no importance one way or the other. Incidentally, however, it may interest the reader to learn that the copyright of this work, which must have earned a fortune during the twenty-five years or so that it has been a 'best-seller', was sold outright by the composer for the sum of about £5.

While we are on the subject it will be appropriate to consider here a few other works of a similar kind which seem to cause considerable distress to many who are otherwise only too ready to appreciate whole-heartedly the art of Sibelius. I refer particularly to the various waltzes—'chevaleresque', 'romantique', 'lyrique', and what not—some for orchestra and some for piano, which are to be found scattered in profusion throughout his work, both late and early. How, it is frequently asked, could the composer of the great symphonies and symphonic poems lower himself to such an extent as to write mere commonplace waltzes such as these? This is not the proper place to consider the question in its widest aspect; I propose to do so in the last chapter when dealing with his work as a whole. For the present it is enough to say that I used to be rather puzzled by it myself, until one evening, when dining with the composer at a restaurant in Helsingfors, I noted with surprise and commented upon the frequency with which the orchestra would play waltzes of Johann Strauss instead of the usual jazz, which, in Finland, is of a peculiarly virulent and pungent type. Sibelius smiled expansively. 'That is because I am here,' he replied; 'they play it because they know how much I love it.' Sibelius, in fact, and not by any means alone among distinguished composers—Brahms and Richard Strauss are two other examples which occur to one in this connexion—cherishes an ardent affection for the Viennese waltz, and particularly for its greatest master, Johann Strauss the younger. These waltzes which he writes in such abundance are to be regarded as a kind of 'Hommage à Strauss', and I believe one would please him more by saying that they were worthy to be compared with those of the master than by praising any of his other works.

The influence of Johann Strauss, moreover, is not confined to the waltzes themselves, but can be detected throughout his work in the form of a strong predilection for themes which make use of the characteristic technical device of the Viennese waltz called the *atempause*—the strongly marked rest, like a catch in the breath, which precedes the final note of the bar. Examples of this peculiarity are to be found in the initial movement of the Symphony no. 1 in E minor, immediately after the statement of the principal subject; in the second theme of the first movement of the Violin Concerto; in the bridge passage linking the scherzo to the finale in the Symphony no. 2—to mention only three instances out of many.

This Viennese element in his music is probably due in part to direct influences sustained during his student days in the Austrian capital, but also indirectly, no doubt, to the nostalgia for the south to which many, if not most, artists of northern provenance have been subject. Another and more familiar aspect of it is perhaps to be found in his cult of the Greek and Latin classics, to which reference has already been made in an earlier chapter, and which receives musical expression in several compositions of which the most important are the early 'Impromptu', set to words by the Swedish poet Rydberg, for female chorus and orchestra, op. 19, and the late 'Oceanides', a tone-poem for large orchestra, op. 73.

The former is not, perhaps, among the most significant or characteristic works of Sibelius, but it is a most admirable expression of the spirit of the poem—a rapturous Dionysian hymn in praise of youth, grace, beauty, and the joys of living, not untinged, however, with a sense of the pathos of the transience and brevity of all mortal things. Its light, fleeting twelve-four and six-four rhythms bear the music and words along in a ceaseless flow from beginning to end, as a river runs to the sea and life ebbs to its goal in death—a perfect musical embodiment of the πάντα ῥεῖ of Heracleitan philosophy.

'The Oceanides' is scored for full modern orchestra, including two harps and four kettledrums (requiring two players), but with the exception of the tremendous climax near the close of the work—strikingly similar in character to that in 'Tapiola', by the way—its resources are used not for the purpose of achieving great sonority but for effects and combinations of the greatest delicacy and subtlety. Those many critics who think of Sibelius as a 'primitive' artist exclusively should study this score, which is of quite exceptional complexity and refinement. The orchestral technique in this work is strikingly different from that encountered in any other of Sibelius, and consists in a kind of *pointillisme* not dissimilar, superficially, from that of the later orchestral compositions of Debussy, such as 'La Mer' and 'Iberia'. It is a piece of pure impressionism, in fact, yet it is in no sense derivative, but on the contrary as highly personal as anything he has written. In 'The Oceanides' Sibelius has taken over the French Impressionist technique and—what no other composer has so far succeeded in doing—has made it entirely his own, and not merely a reflection or distortion of Debussy. He extends its scope, moreover. The French masters of the method and their imitators in other countries confined their attention for the most part to an exploitation of the possibilities afforded by the upper reaches of the orchestral register, and to the attainment, principally, of effects of brilliance and luminosity. Debussy's writing for the lower instruments, and for the double-basses in particular, is as a general rule timid and conventional in comparison with his treatment of the higher instruments, as a result, doubtless, of his exaggerated fear of thickness of texture. In 'The Oceanides' Sibelius has explored the lower depths of the orchestra more thoroughly than any one had previously done, and applied the impressionist method of scoring to the bass instruments, thereby achieving effects of sonority hitherto unknown. Except in a few odd bars here and there the double-basses are dissociated from the 'cellos and play an entirely independent role; the kettledrums are constantly employed, though always *piano*, in playing chords of every kind— major seconds, minor thirds, fifths, and sixths—and altogether the lower octaves of the orchestral compass are written for in a most daring and unconventional manner. With all its subtlety and complexity of instrumental detail, however, the fundamental structure of the music is simple, being almost entirely based on the wood-wind theme heard at the beginning. And for all its daring and modernity of method, the underlying spirit of the work is that of classical antiquity.

Other compositions belonging to this 'classical' group are the 'Song of the Athenians' for men's and boys' voices, seven horns, and percussion, 'The Dryad', op. 45, no. 1, and 'Pan and Echo', a dance intermezzo, op. 53, both for ordinary orchestra. All are attractive works in their way, but hardly important enough to call for detailed examination in a study of this size.

In all the foregoing works we find Sibelius momentarily identifying himself with diverse alien cultural traditions. Beginning with Sweden and visiting in turn Belgium, Germany, England, Austria, Greece, the East, he succeeds in adapting himself to the requirements of each with a quite remarkable and chameleon-like aptitude and facility. In precisely the same way he shows himself capable of practising consummately in any and every kind of purely musical form.

'Night Ride and Sunrise', for example, is an admirable specimen of the type of symphonic poem which was in vogue everywhere during the last decade of the nineteenth century and the first of the twentieth. It is thoroughly conventional in the sense that it is exactly what one would expect it to be from the title. The first thing that would occur to any composer to whom the idea for the work had presented itself would be to establish a regular, headlong, galloping, trochaic metre, and to repeat it indefinitely. This is precisely what Sibelius does, and he keeps it going for over three hundred bars without interruption. But whereas other composers, having found their formula, would be content to repeat it again and again integrally, or nearly so, as for example in the 'Walkürenritt', Sibelius varies his with immense resource throughout. It only becomes a pattern while it serves for a short time as a background to other themes. The 'sunrise' section, again, is superficially very much the same as most other musical sunrises, but with the important difference that it gives the impression of having been inspired by actual experience, whereas in most other cases one feels that the composer has never in his life got up early enough or gone to bed late enough to observe the phenomenon for himself, but has merely slavishly followed the conventional procedure of other composers. That of Sibelius, in fact, is felt and directly observed, *en plein air*; those of others are mere studio pieces, written primarily in order to display their powers of writing effectively for the brass.

The 'In Memoriam' funeral march, op. 59, written about the same time, is another example of precisely the same thing. All the conventional appurtenances of mourning are here, complete in every detail, with an *ostinato* rhythm in the percussion, demisemiquaver figures in the lowest register of the violins, a wailing theme for the wood-wind which breaks into chromatics as a voice breaks with emotion, and so on. Nevertheless one feels again that it is not simply music derived from other music, but the outcome of a definite spiritual experience. The composer has not merely said to himself one morning 'Let us write a funeral march', but has been impelled to do so as the result of a genuine bereavement, a personal loss, a great affliction. In consequence it is a profoundly moving work. Again one is amazed to observe, as in the 'storm' music of 'The Tempest', the 'Night Ride and Sunrise', and so many other works of Sibelius, his power of endowing a stale and hackneyed convention with fresh meaning and new life. He always does the obvious and the expected, but seldom fails to transform it in the process into something entirely novel and original.

The most admirable feature of the Concerto for violin and orchestra, op. 47, written about the same time as the two foregoing works, is probably the happy mean it strikes between brilliance and virtuosity on the one hand, and exclusively intrinsic musical interest on the other. The definition of a concerto given in Grove's *Dictionary of Music and Musicians* is 'the name generally given to an instrumental composition designed to show the skill of an executant', and this must always remain the essential feature and *raison d'être* of the form. At the same time it is no longer enough to do this and nothing else. It is a significant fact that no concerto composed by a superlatively accomplished violinist has yet been able to maintain itself in the repertory; it is equally true that it is rare to find a good violin concerto that has been written by a composer without any practical acquaintance with the instrument. (Brahms, it must be remembered, who might perhaps be considered an exception to the rule, enjoyed the advice and assistance of Joachim in writing the solo part of his concerto, and even so it is not entirely satisfactory.) The best violin concertos, in fact, have practically all been written by composers who have studied the instrument without, however, becoming eminent *virtuosi*, and the fact that Sibelius fulfils this primary condition is probably a partial explanation at least of his success in handling this most exacting form. The solo part, if exceedingly difficult, is nevertheless brilliant and effective, while the level of purely musical interest is correspondingly high.

The form is simple and concise throughout, besides being distinctly original. The exposition in the first movement, for example, is tripartite instead of dual as usual, and the *cadenza* precedes the development section, which is at the same time a recapitulation; the slow second movement consists chiefly in the gradual unfolding, like a flower, of a long, sweet, *cantabile* melody first presented by the solo instrument and then by the orchestra; and the last movement is almost entirely made up of the alternation of two main themes. This variety, combined with simplicity and concision, of formal structure, constitutes one of the chief attractions of the work.

It might perhaps be added that the Concerto, unlike most of the works considered in the present chapter, but in common with the music of 'Pelléas', has occasionally a perceptibly national flavour. Some of the thematic material, indeed, notably the B flat minor episode in the first movement and the second subject of the last, with the characteristic falling fourth in both, is strikingly akin in idiom to Finnish folk-songs of a certain type. Needless to say, however, there is no suggestion here of any deliberate employment of local colour; the resemblance is no doubt entirely unconscious and unintentional.

The two 'Serenades' for violin and medium-sized orchestra, op. 69, are not serenades in either the ancient or the modern sense of the word; that is to say, they do not consist either of a string of short movements, as do those of the first type, neither are they to be regarded as passionate addresses to a lady on a balcony by moonlight, as are those of the second. They are in single movements only, and in form and style resemble minia-ture concertos more than anything else. Their dis-tinctive feature consists in the employment of subject-matter of the most ordinary kind in a peculiarly personal manner. If one considers the themes of either apart from their contexts they seem colourless and undistinguished to the verge of mediocrity, but the treatment they receive, and the scoring in particular, is curiously unlike what one would naturally have expected. The concluding D major chord of the first 'Serenade', for example, is scored for nothing but solo violin, two clarinets in the chalumeau register, double-basses (without 'cellos), and kettledrum on the third of the chord— the low F sharp, although the tonic is available on the other drum. This is a minute point, perhaps, but it is characteristic of the works as a whole, for there is hardly a bar of them in which some curious harmonic or instrumental twist cannot be discerned. Another interesting and typical example of this is to be found in the mysterious intrusion of a soft pedal C sharp for the double-basses and drums upon the G minor harmonies in the first part of the second 'Serenade'. It sounds like a premonition of coming events, and such indeed it is, for the subsequent plot of the work consists largely in the juxtaposition and alternation of the keys of G minor and C sharp minor. In the same way, it may be observed, Beethoven introduces the same foreign note abruptly into the midst of the diatonic F major harmonies in the last movement of the Eighth Symphony, and subsequently proceeds to naturalize it, so to speak. The concluding part of the second 'Serenade', incidentally, with its jerky, insistent, trochaic rhythm, has a distinct affinity to the *finale* of the violin Concerto.

Besides these 'Serenades' Sibelius has also written a large number of smaller works for violin solo with various combinations of instruments, of which six are named 'Humoresques'. In the second the soloist is accompanied by two horns, kettledrums, and strings; in the third by twenty-two strings divided into twelve parts; in the fifth by two flutes, two clarinets, two bassoons, and strings; in the sixth by the same combination without the clarinets. The most interesting of these violin and orchestral miniatures, however, are the two pieces of op. 77—'Laetare anima mea' and 'Devotion' (*Ab imo pectore*)— scored respectively for two flutes, clarinet, two horns, four kettledrums (two players), harp, and strings, and for two flutes, clarinet, two bassoons, four horns, three trombones, and strings, in addition to the solo instrument.

The chief attraction of all these little works lies not so much in their intrinsic musical interest, which is frequently slight and sometimes even less than that, as in the skill with which the composer handles unusual combinations of instruments, and in the delicate and subtle shades of tone-colour these afford.

For violin and piano there exist several sets of pieces amongst which those of op. 79 are particularly brilliant and effective. For 'cello and piano there would seem to be only one published composition, and that a fairly early one, entitled 'Malinconia', op. 20—a solid, powerful piece of work, but rather lacking in distinction and in no way representative of the composer at his best, and on the whole this may be said to apply to all the works we have just been considering, with the possible exception of the two pieces, op. 77, for violin and small orchestra. Whatever their merits or demerits considered abstractly, however, it must at least be admitted that the writing for the solo stringed instrument in all of them is masterly. The same, unfortunately, cannot be said of the sets of piano pieces which Sibelius has poured forth in such profusion at every period of his career, amounting to over one hundred numbers in all. Not only are they for the most part completely undistinguished in conception and musical substance, but they are also singularly ineffective from the point of view of the instrument.

This in itself need not surprise us. A feeling for the piano as a medium of expression seldom goes together with a feeling for other instrumental *media*, but is generally found in inverse ratio to it.

The greatest composers for the piano, such as Chopin and Schumann, are notorious for their feeble handling of the orchestra, while the greatest masters of the orchestra, speaking from a purely technical point of view, such as Berlioz, Wagner, and Strauss, are as a rule curiously inept and insensitive in their writing for the piano on the rare occasions when they attempt it. It is precisely the same with Sibelius, who is primarily a master of the orchestra; indeed, his piano writing is distinctly reminiscent of that of Berlioz.

His weakness in this department, then, need not, as I have said, surprise us; it is only what one would naturally have expected. What is surprising, however, is that he should have written so much for an instrument which he does not seem to understand, and even appears positively to dislike and despise. A curious feature of his piano works viewed as a whole, moreover, is that, so far from there being any discernible process of development from early ones to late, the contrary rather is the truth. The remark already quoted from Grove's *Dictionary of Music and Musicians*, to the effect that 'the latest piano pieces are no better than, and not essentially different from, the first six impromptus', is an under-statement even, for actually the early piano sonata, op. 8, the 'Ten Pieces', op. 24, the 'Kyllikki' pieces, op. 41, are on the whole very much more interesting than anything he has subsequently written for the instrument, and the latest volumes are definitely the weakest. On the other hand, when the piano is restricted to the subordinate role of accompaniment, either to stringed instrument or to voice, Sibelius's treatment of it is generally quite felicitous, if somewhat undistinguished.

The songs, of which there are nearly a hundred, represent a very much more important side of his creative activity, but they also exhibit somewhat puzzling features when viewed as a whole. In the first place they are curiously unequal; within each opus number admirable examples are found side by side with others markedly inferior, and again it might be true to say that the latest songs of op. 88 and 90 'are no better than, and not essentially different from' those of op. 13 and 17. Between the two extremes of early and late, however, one finds many examples superior to those at either of them.

So far as the first songs are concerned, they cannot be compared in any way with the work Sibelius was producing in other forms at the same time. Beside such things as 'En Saga' or 'The

Swan of Tuonela' even the best of them, such as
'To Fricka', op. 13, no. 6, or 'The Dragon-fly',
op. 17, no. 5, seem timid and conventional in
comparison. With op. 35 a great advance is to be
perceived. No. 1, 'Jubal', shows a definite step
forward in respect of plasticity and subtlety of workmanship, while no. 2, 'Theodora', is a masterpiece.
The poem by Gripenberg on the Thamar-like
motive of the Empress Theodora, 'ardent and faith-
less, aflame with a passion consuming and fierce',
whose favours ultimately bring ruin and death to
their recipient, has inspired Sibelius to a musical
utterance of exceptional power and originality.

From then onwards groups of songs follow in
rapid succession, many of their numbers being on
a very high level indeed. Op. 38, nos. 1, 2, and 3,
'Autumn Night', 'On a Balcony by the Sea', and
'In the Night', are particularly fine, the other two
of the set being more in the earlier manner. Op. 50
and 57 on the whole maintain the advance if they
do not extend it. Op. 50, nos. 3 and 5, 'A Maiden
yonder sings' and 'The silent Town', are excellent
pieces of tone-painting in miniature, and the songs
of the latter group, if not outstanding, reveal on
the whole a more elaborate and refined craftsmanship than hitherto, especially in the accompani-

ments. Op. 60, no. 1, a setting of Shakespeare's 'Come away, Death', is a perfect little song. It is only unfortunate that the music is set to a Swedish translation, the accentuation of which does not exactly correspond with the English original, since an English singer is faced with the awkward necessity of altering the poet's text or else not singing it at all. But since the English singer adopts the second alternative in any case, the problem does not arise. Op. 60, no. 2, also a Shakespeare setting, of 'When that I was', is good, but not so good as its fellow.

Op. 61, in my opinion, represents the highest point to which Sibelius attains as a song-writer. No praise could be too great for such admirable lyrics as no. 1, 'Slow as the Colours', with its subtle cross-rhythms and finely moulded voice part; no. 2, 'Lapping Waters', with its murmuring single-part figure for the piano; no. 3, 'When I dream', with its long declamatory opening and restrained accompaniment; and nos. 4 and 5 with their ingenious repetition and variation of the same motives throughout in different keys. The remaining three numbers of the set, if hardly on the same high level, are nevertheless well above the average.

Of the six songs which make up op. 72 the first

couple have either not been published or are out of print—whichever the reason, I have not been able to see them. Subject to this qualification, the set is not up to the standard of the preceding one, with the possible exception of no. 6, 'A Hundred Ways', which is certainly a fine song. The group constituting op. 86 are slight and uninteresting, and although the songs of op. 88 are charming miniatures, especially the exquisite last number, 'Blommans öde', and the first two of op. 90 are well above the rest, these later songs are definitely disappointing as a whole when we consider the great music that the composer was producing at the same time in other forms, and represent a distinct falling-off in comparison with earlier essays in the same category.

Neither in his early nor in his late period, in fact, are the songs of Sibelius on the same level as his best work in other directions, but only in his middle period. In other words, while in his finest and most inspired orchestral compositions a definite line of progress can be discerned, while in his miscellaneous and occasional work much the same consistent level is maintained throughout, and while in his piano music a definite retrogression can be observed, his lyrical output, viewed in broad outline, describes a curve, rising up to a point and falling again. This curve, moreover, coincides with the degree of the composer's preoccupation with the form. In his earliest period he produced only two groups, op. 13 and 17; between op. 35 and 61 there are no fewer than eight sets of songs which contain practically all of his best specimens; and from op. 62 onwards, right up to op. 116, which is the composer's total at the time of writing, only four more groups appear, of which the last is no later than op. 90.

It is interesting to note, too, that the majority of his best songs are essentially nature pictures and moods, with the human element, where present, in the background. In settings of love lyrics and so forth he is seldom completely successful, though an exception might perhaps be made in favour of the early 'To Fricka' already mentioned. For the most part his essays in this direction lack sensitiveness, and sometimes even border dangerously on the banal and the commonplace. Sibelius, in short, is not primarily a lyricist; his chief strength resides elsewhere. A handful of the songs of his middle period are wholly admirable, but for the rest only isolated numbers here and there can be placed beside his best work in other fields.

In view of his intense, almost exclusive, pre-occupation with chamber music in his early years, it is not a little curious that Sibelius should have subsequently neglected it entirely with the exception of one string quartet, 'Voces Intimae', op. 56, belonging to his middle period. What makes it all the more unaccountable is the fact that this isolated specimen is such a very fine one. It consists of five shortish movements: a short *andante* leading to *allegro moderato, vivace, adagio di molto, allegretto* (*ma pesante*), and a final *allegro*.

The most striking feature of the work as a whole is the extreme prevalence of conjunct motion—almost the entire thematic material of all five movements is built up from fragments of scale passages. Sibelius, in fact, has woven the texture of this music out of the basic facts of musical experience, as it were, the eternal commonplaces. There are no grand, sweeping themes in it, no clearly distinguishable first and second subjects in any of the movements, except in the lyrical third. For the rest one can only speak of a first subject in the sense that it is the first to make its appearance; the time-honoured implications of the expression are no longer valid here. In the first movement, for example, three subjects in the main key follow each other in swift succession at the very outset, none of which can claim precedence or superior rank over either of the others. The old classic order, with its first and second themes as king and queen respectively, and the rest of the thematic material as their humble subjects, gives place here to a kind of ideal democracy in which all are equal and share alike in the construction of each movement—except, as I have already said, for the third, which has a definite chief theme.

This equality of subject-matter is, of course, largely the outcome of the predominance of conjunct motion, which also creates so strong an impression of unity between all the constituent movements of the work that one is at first inclined to believe that there is sometimes a definite interchange of themes between them. This is not so, however. Phrases can certainly be found in one movement which strongly resemble some in others, but when the context is carefully examined it will be seen that each of them grows naturally and inevitably out of its surroundings and is in no way a harking-back to what has gone before, or an anticipation of what is to come. Altogether, this work ranks with the finest achievements of Sibelius's middle period. Why it should be so conspicuously

neglected by quartets, in this country at least, is
a mystery, for quite apart from its intrinsic merits,
it is beautifully written for the medium and exceedingly effective in performance.

III. THE SYMPHONIES

IN the two preceding chapters the various separate aspects of Sibelius's art have been briefly reviewed, from choral and orchestral works on a large scale down to simple lyrics and dances; we now turn our attention to his achievements in the formal category which may in a sense be said to contain and embrace them all, namely, the symphony. For, taking it simply in its most ordinary and conventional aspect, in the form of the customary four movements consecrated by classical usage—the first, with its intricate plot and predominantly intellectual appeal; the second, generally of a lyrical, subjective, and expressive nature; the third, essentially a dance movement of some kind or another; the fourth, broad, epic, and heroic in character—the symphony is a compendium and epitome of all musical forms and styles and modes of thought.

Hence it is that symphony constitutes the most formidable and searching all-round test of musicianship that can possibly be devised. It is as if one were to require of a writer that he be a superlative dramatist and choreographer, a lyric and an epic poet, all in one and at the same time—a demand which probably only Shakespeare and Goethe in modern times could even potentially satisfy, and, not surprisingly, the number of composers who similarly excel in every conceivable direction is hardly if at all larger.

The reason for this is, of course, that to a great extent the necessary qualities are mutually exclusive. It is a truism, for instance, that the greatest lyricists are seldom equally pre-eminent in constructions on a large scale, and vice versa; and even on the rare occasions when the two faculties are found combined in a single artist they do not often coincide in point of time, but are generally in the ascendant at different stages of his development. The lyric and choric gifts, in fact, belong essentially to youth, constructive ability on a large scale to age. Beethoven is probably the only example there is of a composer who carried over the former, undiminished in strength and unimpaired in quality, into his maturity; Mozart the only one to exhibit in comparative youth the constructive powers which as a rule come only late in life. If only for this reason these two must be accounted the supreme and unequalled symphonists of all time.

It is not enough, in fact, to be able to excel in one or two directions, however greatly. In sym-

phony not even the combination of the highest
intellect and the deepest emotion will suffice. When
Brahms once ruefully observed that 'to write a
symphony is no laughing matter', he was assuredly
right in a sense, but profoundly wrong in another.
A symphony should be a laughing matter at times,
in the true sense of the words, just as much as it
should be a serious one at others. 'Dulce est desi-
pere in loco,' and nowhere more so than in a symphony, which is a mirror of the complete man, a
microcosm of human experience. The wisdom and
understanding of age, the energy and vitality of
maturity, the lyricism and passionate intensity of
youth, the artless gaiety and spontaneity of child-
hood—all these are necessary to the complete
symphonist. As in Carlo Gozzi's fable of the
Princess Turandot, who could only be won by him
who was able to answer correctly each of the
riddles she propounded, the penalty of failure in
even one of them alone being death, so the composer who aspires to mastership of the symphony
must succeed in satisfying us in every possible
direction. In so far as he falls short in one of them
he fails altogether, and the history of music is
littered with the forgotten names of innumerable
composers who have rashly courted symphonic

favours and have been found wanting in one way or another.

It is perfectly true, of course, that a composer is under no obligation to observe strictly the classical four-movement formula. There is no reason whatever why a good symphony should not on occasion dispense entirely with a lyrical slow movement, or a *scherzo*, or, for that matter, with any or even all of the familiar convention. There is not even any restriction on the number of movements it may contain. Rubinstein's 'Ocean Symphony', if I remember rightly, consists of no fewer than seven, but if it is a bad symphony it is not on that account; and Sibelius himself, as we shall see, has written one, his seventh, in a single movement, which is none the less a great symphony. The fact remains, however, that a composer's rank as a symphonist depends chiefly on the extent to which he is able to satisfy the most diverse and opposite requirements, and the conventional four-movement scheme to which reference has been made is merely a convenient symbol of this. A large work in several slow movements, for example, or a succession of dance movements, might be excellent considered simply as music but would not constitute a good symphony; diversity, contrast, opposition, are the primary and fundamental laws of its being.

In view of the exacting nature of the form it is not surprising to find that none of the outstanding landmarks in its history has been created early in the life of any composer, with the exception of Mozart—the exception to every rule.[1] Beethoven was thirty and Brahms forty before they made their first attempts, and none of the early specimens of Haydn, Schubert, Mendelssohn, or Schumann is of primary importance, or in any way comparable to their achievements in other directions at the same stage of their respective careers. Sibelius is one of those who wisely refrained from measuring their strength with the symphony until they had arrived at a certain degree of maturity. His first attempt, op. 39 in E minor, was written at the age of thirty-four, after he had already attained to complete mastery in other forms.

It is a longish work lasting approximately forty minutes in performance, consisting of the regular four movements of the classical tradition, and it is scored for the ordinary full orchestra including bass tuba and harp. The character and internal construc-

---

[1] The 'Symphonie Fantastique' of Berlioz, written at the age of twenty-five, is undoubtedly a magnificent and arresting work, but hardly a model of symphonic form, which is all I am speaking of here.

tion of each individual movement is similarly orthodox and straightforward. The first exhibits conformity to the triune principle of exposition,
development, and recapitulation, and the chief roles
in the unfolding of the action are confided to the
customary first and second subjects, the one virile
and energetic, the other suave and gentle, each with
a subsidiary theme in attendance. In the second
movement the roles are reversed as usual, the chief
theme being a tranquil and expressive *cantabile*
melody with a strenuous counter-subject; the third
is a characteristically vivacious *scherzo* with a
strongly contrasted trio, and the last (*quasi una
fantasia*), with its long, dominating principal subject winding its way to a triumphant apotheosis, is
a typical example of the orthodox *finale*.

As in form, so in substance and in style it is
somewhat conventional, and certainly a much less
personal work than many others he had already
written. One notes in particular a strong Russian
influence here and there, especially in the thematic
material, which is unusual in his work. The first
subject of the initial movement, for example, is
strikingly akin to that in the first movement of
Borodin's symphony in E flat major, only sharpened
and intensified; that of the second movement is

distinctly reminiscent of Tchaikovsky, and the broad, sweeping theme of the *finale* is very much the kind of theme one finds in the last movements of Rachmaninoff or Glazounoff, only very much better. At the same time, however, the substratum is national; in fact one may say that if the principal subjects are predominantly Slavonic in character, the subsidiary ones are often distinctively Finnish, and the atmosphere of storm and conflict which pervades the entire work is largely the outcome of a kind of revolt on the part of this thematic rank and file against their lords and masters. In this way the symphony presents a symbolical picture of Finnish insurrection against Russian tyranny and oppression. Not that I would suggest for a moment that the composer had any such purpose in mind while writing it, but there would be nothing surprising in it if there were an unconscious correspondence between the state of mind of the composer and the position of his unhappy country at the time when the symphony was conceived, at the very height of the Tsarist persecution. On the contrary, it would be surprising if there were not.

Taken as a whole the symphony is a work of quite outstanding merit. It may not, as I have said, be a particularly individual production, but one can think of no one else who could have written it. It is in the same *genre* and tradition as the symphonies of Tchaikovsky, Glazounoff, Dvořák, and many similar composers, but it stands head and shoulders above all of them in thematic distinction and formal cohesion, and in no way below them in respect of brilliance and certainty of orchestration. Sibelius, in fact, begins where they leave off.

With the Symphony no. 2 in D major, written three years later, an immense advance is to be perceived. If the First is the very archetype of the romantic, picturesque symphony of the latter part of the nineteenth century, the Second strikes out a new path altogether. The first is a conclusion, the last of its dynasty and in many ways the best; the second is the beginning of a new line, and contains the germs of immense and fruitful developments. In addition, apart from an occasional suggestion of the influence of Tchaikovsky, it is entirely personal and original in idiom from beginning to end.

The Second Symphony is scored for the same orchestra as its predecessor, minus the harp, and is slightly shorter. In outward appearance it still conforms to the traditional four-movement formula of *allegro, andante, scherzo,* and *finale,* but the internal organization of the movements reveals

134

many important innovations, amounting at times, and particularly in the first movement, to a veritable revolution, and to the introduction of an entirely new principle into symphonic form. The nature of this revolution can be best described by saying that whereas in the symphony of Sibelius's predecessors the thematic material is generally introduced in an exposition, taken to pieces, dissected, and analysed in a development section, and put together again in a recapitulation, Sibelius in the first movement of the Second Symphony inverts the process, introducing thematic fragments in the exposition, building them up into an organic whole in the development section, then dispersing and dissolving the material back into its primary constituents in a brief recapitulation. Furthermore, the convention of first and second subjects or groups of subjects is abandoned; in this movement one can detect several distinct groups of thematic germs none of which can claim the right to be regarded as the most important.

Nothing in the entire literature of symphonic form is more remarkable than the way in which Sibelius here presents a handful of seemingly disconnected and meaningless scraps of melody, and then breathes life into them, bringing them into organic relation with each other and causing them to grow in stature and significance with each successive appearance, like living things.[1]

The slow second movement is also highly individual. The familiar principle of the contrast between a lyrical chief subject and a more virile second subject is here intensified into an almost epic conflict, involving several groups of thematic protagonists. The melancholy, reflective first subject is quite unequal to the task of coping with the violent opposition it arouses, and is compelled to call to its assistance a second lyrical subject which, in its turn, engenders antagonism. The melodic writing in this movement, incidentally, is of quite exceptional beauty, particularly the second lyrical subject, which is both exquisitely moulded and deeply expressive.

The bustling *scherzo* is comparatively conventional in form and style, apart from the lovely *trio* which is built upon a theme beginning with no fewer than nine repetitions of the same note—a thing no one but Sibelius would dare or could afford

[1] A particularly striking and instructive example of this is afforded by the theme given out by the wood-wind on the second part of p. 8 of the full score (letter C). At its first appearance it seems entirely insignificant, but with each repetition or variation it develops and expands until at last it overshadows all.

to do. For the rest it is on familiar lines, and the concluding movement which follows without a break is in the usual *finale* tradition—broad, stately, ceremonious, rather pompous perhaps here and there. In these days of cynicism and disillusion it is of course the fashion to sneer at the convention of the 'happy ending', of which the orthodox symphonic *finale* is the musical equivalent, and it is certainly true that most modern attempts to conform to it ring hollow and insincere. We of the present generation simply do not feel like that; we find it difficult to be triumphant, and we have no doubt excellent reasons for it. The fact remains that it is a weakness and a deficiency in us, and there is something of sour grapes in the contemporary attitude towards those artists of an earlier generation who have achieved the state of spiritual serenity, optimism, and repose which makes it possible for them to conclude a work convincingly in this manner. Sibelius is one of them; his triumphant final movements, so far from being due to a mere unthinking acceptance of a formal convention, correspond to a definite spiritual reality.

The Symphony no. 3 in C major, op. 52, was written in 1905–7 and consists of three movements only—two *allegro* movements with a middle one which is neither an *andante* nor a *scherzo* but partakes to a certain extent of both. Apart from the decrease in the number of movements, each of the three is distinctly shorter than those of either of its predecessors. The difference in dimensions between the Third and the First and Second is roughly indicated by the number of pages in the full scores—160 in the First, 145 in the Second, only 70 in the Third. The comparative brevity of the latter is further enhanced by the fact that it contains no slow movement, strictly speaking.

Together with this diminution both in total length and in the size of the individual movements, a similar tendency is to be observed in the orchestral means employed. Firstly, the bass tuba, which played a prominent role in both of the preceding symphonies, is omitted; secondly, a most noticeable degree of economy and restraint is to be observed throughout in the scoring. In the First and Second Symphonies the wind, and especially the brass, seems to dominate; in the Third the strings definitely take precedence. The trumpets and trombones in particular, which play a very conspicuous part in the proceedings of the earlier symphonies, here recede into the background whence they emerge only on special occasions. The texture in general is very much lighter in every way, the style more sensitive, supple, and discreet. Similarly, the formal complexity which characterized the first two movements of the Second Symphony give way in the corresponding movements of the Third to a quite exceptional clarity and simplicity. In place of the multiplicity of themes in the initial movement of the Second one finds a reversion to the classical principle of two main subjects, each with an attendant satellite figuration, and the plot is simple, precise, clear-cut, and distinguished by extreme economy of material; while the second movement is, if possible, even simpler and more straightforward, consisting as it does in little else but the ringing of the changes upon a single theme by shifting it up and down on to different degrees of the diatonic scale. The last movement alone, or at any rate the first part of it, reveals a certain formal complexity. As in the first movement of the Second, several disjointed and in themselves insignificant little figures are announced at the outset and gradually welded together into a logical and coherent tissue in masterly fashion. The second section of the movement, however, consists for the most part, like the preceding movement, in ringing a series of melodic and harmonic changes upon a strongly marked, persistent rhythmical figure—a method of procedure which, from now onwards, becomes a distinctive feature of Sibelius's symphonic style.

In feeling and atmosphere, too, the Third Symphony presents a striking contrast with its two forerunners. The sombre, restless tone of the first, the strenuous and impassioned character of the second, give way to a mood of unclouded serenity and sunny gaiety, particularly exemplified in the delightful middle movement, which is perhaps the most attractive and original of the three.

An even more striking contrast, however, is that afforded by a comparison of the Third and the Fourth, in A minor, op. 63. It is difficult, indeed, to believe that the same composer could have written both; one only knows that no one else would have been capable of writing either of them. They seem, in fact, to belong to entirely different worlds and to have nothing in common with each other, but each of them, none the less, expresses a definite aspect of their creator's complex personality, and both are equally individual utterances in their different ways.

In contradistinction to the bright and cheerful mood of the Third, the prevailing mood of the

Fourth is one of the deepest tragedy and gloom, while its formal structure is as elusive and baffling as that of the Third is simple and easily grasped. In style, too, the contrast is equally striking. In place of the definite, clear-cut, self-contained themes, the plain diatonic harmonies and vigorous elementary rhythms of the earlier work, we get for the most part tiny, pregnant thematic germs only, a harmonic idiom at times so strange and recondite that it cannot even be defined as atonal, and a prevalence of twisted, dislocated rhythms and syncopations. The only feature the two works share in common is the tendency to spareness both in length and in breadth, as it were, both in dimensions and in texture, and the same marked restraint in the employment of the orchestral forces. The Third Symphony, we have already seen, was less than half the length of its two predecessors and its texture had similarly undergone a drastic process of clarification and refinement, but the Fourth goes even further in these directions. If the Third represents the result of a slimming treatment, a reduction of the adipose tissues and somewhat opulent curves of the symphonic muse as she appears in the first two examples, the Fourth is the outcome of a process of sheer starvation, of a fakir-like asceticism and self-denial. The Fourth Symphony is gaunt, spectral, emaciated almost; the question here is no longer one of superfluous flesh, but of any flesh at all—the very bones protrude.

Take, for example, the first movement—unusual, by the way, if not unique, in being a *quasi adagio* constructed, in broad outline, according to the accepted principles of the classic first-movement formula. The initial four notes merely, embracing a compass of an augmented fourth within the duration of no more than three crotchets, constitute the leading theme and principal thematic germ of the whole movement; the exposition is over by p. 5 of the full score, the development section by p. 10, and the whole movement itself by p. 13. It is unquestionably the most compact and concise movement in symphonic literature. One can think of no other which says so much in such a small space, in so short a time. This applies equally to the second movement, an *allegro molto vivace*, occupying no more than 15 pages and consequently lasting an even shorter time than the first; also to the third, a *largo*, in which a theme is built up out of nothing before our eyes within the space of no more than 9 pages of full score. Only the last movement is on a scale commensurate with that of most ordinary symphonic movements, and even this is equally tightly packed with substance and lacking in any superfluity of tissue.

With all this terseness, however, one does not feel that anything essential has been omitted. The Fourth Symphony may be small in size but it is great in weight. Physicists and astronomers tell us that there is in the cosmos a species of star, which they call a White Dwarf, the substance of which is so dense and compressed that a piece the size of a shilling may weigh as much as several tons, and, Sibelius's Fourth Symphony is a veritable White Dwarf in the musical firmament. It is a landmark, not merely in his own development, but in the history of musical form, representing as it does the farthest point to which the principle of the elimination of non-essentials has been pushed. There is not a superfluous note in the score from beginning to end, and hardly one that is not of thematic origin, although the most careful and minute scrutiny may sometimes be necessary in order to trace the connexion between the theme and its ultimate derivates. Sometimes, indeed, it can only be felt or intuitively apprehended. The scoring, too, is similarly of the utmost restraint and austerity throughout. The modest instrumental requirements of the Third are here still further reduced by the omission of a third trumpet, and only in a few bars in the whole work is the full orchestra employed, the greater part of the action being carried out by a bare handful of instruments.

The complete absence of sensuous appeal in this work, coupled with the exacting demands it makes upon the intelligence of audiences, will always prevent it from becoming popular. For the few, however, it probably constitutes Sibelius's greatest achievement; he has certainly never written anything to surpass it.

Once again the next symphony in the series stands at the very opposite pole to its predecessor in almost every respect. In the Fifth Symphony in E flat major, op. 82, there is no trace of the brooding gloom and sombre melancholy which is the spiritual key-note of the Fourth; like the Third, it is a sunny, genial work throughout. The terseness, economy, and extreme concentration of thought, the reticence and sobriety of style which characterizes the former are not to be found in the latter. If the Fourth is a White Dwarf, in fact, the Fifth is its opposite, a Red Giant, a Betelgeuse of music, a huge work in which the substance is highly attenuated and rarefied. The four movements of the former amount to a bare 68 pages of full score, the three of the latter to 136—exactly double. Not that it lasts twice as long in performance; two of the movements of the Fourth are in slow *tempo*, whereas none of those in the Fifth are, but that in itself only serves to emphasize more strongly the profound difference in character between the two works.

The form, too, of all movements of the Fifth is comparatively straightforward, the style broad, simple, and easily understood, the thematic material more definitely melodic, the harmony diatonic and consonant, the rhythms simple and clear-cut, the orchestration rich and sonorous. In the Fourth there is not a bar that could possibly have been written by any other composer, dead or alive—it is a profoundly personal and subjective utterance, from first note to last. In the Fifth, on the contrary, there is not a bar, considered in isolation from its context, that could not have been written by any one else, yet curiously enough the effect of the whole is just as completely and absolutely individual, as utterly unlike anything else in music as the Fourth itself. For this reason it is perhaps an even more remarkable achievement than its predecessor, for it is less difficult—though assuredly difficult enough— to do something which no one else has ever previously done, than to reveal a fresh and un-suspected beauty in the familiar, the obvious, the commonplace, the hackneyed even, which is what Sibelius does in this work.

The very opening is a case in point. The horn theme announced in the first bars, which is the chief theme of the initial movement, might have been written by almost any one—by Brahms, for example, to whose horn theme in the first movement of the D major Symphony it bears a distinct family resemblance. Yet nothing could be more unlike Brahms or, for that matter, any other composer than the treatment it subsequently receives, or the developments to which it gives rise. Again, the second movement consists of a series of variations on a theme which might have occurred to any tenth-rate composer, and would in all probability have been dismissed by him without a second thought as altogether too banal and commonplace to be made use of; yet this movement is one of quite astonishing beauty and originality. Similarly the broad, swinging theme in the last movement, confided on its first appearance to horns and strings, and later to the trumpets, is almost note for note identical with a popular music-hall song of some ten years or so ago, but in Sibelius's hands it is endowed with a grandeur and a dignity that banish entirely from our minds its dubious associations. These are only three examples chosen more or less at random; the score is full of such things. This uncanny power of transforming the most ordinary and even commonplace material into something rich and strange by means of some unexplainable gift of musical alchemy had already been adumbrated in some earlier works, notably the String Quartet and the Serenades for violin and orchestra; it henceforth becomes the dominant characteristic of all Sibelius's music.

The Fifth Symphony constitutes a relaxation from the tension and severe discipline of the Fourth as regards mood, form, and style, but apart from the reinstatement of the third trumpet, which had been dropped in the Third and Fourth, the instrumental forces remain the same. In the Sixth Symphony in D minor, op. 104, the mood is again more subdued, the form more brief and concentrated, the style more sober and restrained; for once, however, the composer permits himself the unwonted luxury of two additions to the frugal and Spartan orchestra with which he had contented himself in his three preceding symphonies, namely, a harp and a bass clarinet.

In spite of this partial relaxation from austerity, however, the scoring in this symphony is by no means rich and opulent. Quite the contrary, indeed, it is noticeably much more restrained than that of its predecessor, though never approaching the starkness and asceticism of the Fourth. In general one may say that the whole character of the Sixth Symphony is that of a midway point between the two opposite extremes touched in the preceding pair. The spiritual and emotional key-note of the work is a sense of poise, serenity, and proportion, which is as far removed from the austerity of the one as it is from the exuberant abandon of the other—the very embodiment, in fact, of the qualities implied in the untranslatable Greek word σωφροσύνη.

The chief interest of the work is formal. In the first movement the conventional tripartite scheme of exposition, development, and recapitulation is abandoned: more accurately, perhaps, while their outlines are broadly discernible they are merged and interfused with each other to such an extent that it is virtually impossible to say where the one begins and the other ends. Moreover, several groups of thematic fragments are introduced instead of the customary two main ones, as in the first movement of the Second Symphony, but at the same time there is nevertheless a definite first subject among them which dominates the rest and is worked out at considerable length in the traditional manner.

In form as in other respects, in fact, this movement is in the nature of a compromise, a *via media*. It represents in a sense a fusion of the classical methods of procedure with the novel principles of construction introduced in some of the composer's earlier symphonies. This suggestion of a balance struck between two extremes is further reflected symbolically in the tonality which is ostensibly that of D minor but with a major sixth (B natural), giving the impression of hovering ambiguously between major and minor. This slightly modal atmosphere—unusual in the music of Sibelius, which is almost always strongly tonal in character—can be perceived to a certain extent in the other movements also.

Another uncommon feature of the work is that it has no slow movement, properly speaking, its place being taken by an *allegretto* of great melodic charm and rhythmical subtlety. Still another is the fact that the *scherzo* has no contrasting *trio* but is all of a piece. Singular, too, and arresting is the way in which all the movements (except the third), after developing in direct and logical fashion throughout, seem suddenly to melt away and dissolve into nothing in their concluding bars.

On the whole it is probably true to say that the Sixth is not one of the most immediately striking or attractive numbers in Sibelius's symphonic sequence. It neither soars to the radiant heights of the Fifth nor plumbs the sombre depths of the Fourth; it has neither the breadth and grandeur of the First and Second nor the fresh charm and sinewy, athletic grace of the Third. Nevertheless, like each of them, it has its own individual qualities which earn for it as secure a place in one's critical estimation as is held by any of them.

Sibelius's Seventh—and up to the time of writing, last—Symphony in C major, op. 105, is in one gigantic movement based in the main upon the same structural principles as the first movement of the Sixth. That is to say, it has one chief dominating subject, a fanfare-like theme which first appears on a solo trombone near the outset and recurs twice, more or less integrally, and in addition a host of small, pregnant, fragmentary motives of which at least a dozen play a prominent part in the unfolding of the action. The resourceful way in which these are varied, developed, juxtaposed, permuted, and combined into a continuous and homogeneous texture is one of the miracles of modern music; Sibelius himself has never done anything to equal it in this respect. If the Fourth represents the highest point to which he attains in the direction of economy of material and concision of form, the Seventh shows him at the summit of his powers in respect of fecundity of invention and subtlety and intricacy of design. It is not merely a consummate masterpiece of formal construction, however, but also a work of great expressive beauty, of a lofty grandeur and dignity, a truly Olympian serenity and repose which are unique in modern music, and, for that matter, in modern art of any kind. It seems, indeed, to belong to a different age altogether, a different order of civilization, a different world almost—the world of classical antiquity.

After this necessarily brief and inadequate examination of Sibelius's symphonies separately and individually, let us now consider them collectively, as a contribution to the history of the form. It will first be necessary, however, to devote a few words to a consideration of the nature of the form itself, *per se*, and of the problems to which it gives rise.

The first question that presents itself is whether,

in view of the vast latitude permitted in works
bearing the designation of symphony, and the immense and fundamental differences that can be
perceived between many of the finest examples so-
called, it can properly be regarded as being a torm
at all in the strict sense of the word. For not merely
is the number and character of the constituent movements entirely arbitrary, but also the formal principles according to which each and all of them are
constructed. A great deal is made in text-books and
programme analyses, for example, of the triune convention of exposition, development, and recapitulation in the first or principal movement, carried out
by first and second subjects or groups of subjects;
but even this, however, is by no means a constant
feature throughout the history of the form, but only
during a certain period of it, and even then extensive modifications of any or all of the structural
features of the scheme were so freely permitted that
no single formula, however vague and generalized,
could possibly be discovered which could apply to
all accepted masterpieces in the form. In fact, as
Professor Tovey has truly observed in one of his
many acute and penetrating contributions to the
Encyclopædia Britannica, 'no design is known to
pure instrumental music that is not possible as the

movement of a sonata,' and sonata is of course, so far as form at least is concerned, synonymous with symphony.

An excellent example, by the way, of the transcendental gibberish written by people who believe in tne existence of a definite formula for symphonic construction is to be found in the statement made somewhere by, if I recollect rightly, Sir Hubert Parry, to the effect that in a certain work of Mozart the second subject appears before the first!

The truth is that symphony is not, and never has been, a form in the sense in which, for instance, the fugue or the sonnet are forms, prescribing as they do certain definite procedures in defiance of which they cease to have any right to the titles at all. No poet would dream of calling a piece of blank verse a hundred lines long a sonnet, but so far as form is concerned practically anything can be called a sonata without violating any law or principle.

Are we to conclude, then, as many people do, that 'symphony' is merely a name which can be conveniently applied to any orchestral composition on a large scale? By no means. It may be impossible to give a satisfactory formal definition of what constitutes a symphony, but the word nevertheless has certain precise implications. It is possible to conceive of two works without a single formal feature in common being both good symphonies; it is possible, also, for two works to resemble each other closely in every structural detail and yet for one of them to be symphonic and the other unsymphonic.

In short, while we may not be able to say positively what a symphony is, we know what we mean by the adjective symphonic. Symphony, in fact, is not a form, but 'symphonic' is a style. We say of a piece of music that it is symphonic in the same way that we speak of a building as Gothic, or Romanesque; it does not tell us anything about the shape, dimensions, or proportions of the work any more than the architectural terms do, but it does convey a very definite sense of the style in which it is written. Let us try to determine the leading features and characteristics of this style.

There was once a French critic, it may be remembered, who roundly condemned the D minor Symphony of César Franck, declaring that it could not properly be regarded as a symphony at all, for the simple reason that the score contained a part for the cor anglais. For this remark the unfortunate critic has ever since been held up to ridicule and contempt as the absolute personification of critical ineptitude and unenlightened pedantry. But is the remark really as absurd as it admittedly seems to be at first sight? I think not. I do not know who the critic was, or anything whatever about him except this one notorious statement of his, but I think it is at least conceivable that he meant something more by it than appears upon the surface. In other words, while it is manifestly ridiculous to deny that it is perfectly possible to write an excellent symphony with a part for cor anglais, it is none the less true that the composer who feels the need for this instrument in a symphony has probably—I put it no higher than that—an unsymphonic mind; the reason being that the nature, the personality so to speak, of the cor anglais is in essence antagonistic to symphonic style, of which the fundamental principle resides in the strict subordination of instrumental personalities to the *ensemble*. The cor anglais is essentially an egoist by nature who must always be in the limelight whatever happens; it is incapable of suppressing its individuality, and has in particular an inveterate propensity for indulging in a vein of romantic and subjective melancholy, *à la mode de* Byron—Childe Harold brooding on the field of Waterloo, or on the Bridge of Sighs at Venice, and so forth—which is at the very opposite pole to the symphonic spirit. Symphonic, in fact, is essentially

155

a classic style—the classical style *par excellence* in music, and any suggestion of the obtrusive, the striking, the excessive, the singular, the abnormal—in a word the romantic—is anathema to it. And though it is no doubt technically possible to write for the cor anglais in such a way that its romantic personality is not unduly obtruded, the fact remains that to do so would involve the contradiction and negation of its character; there would, in fact, be no point in writing for it at all in that case.[1]

It seems to me, then, that our French critic, whether he himself was conscious of the implications of his statement or not, was voicing a profound truth in somewhat epigrammatic and consequently provocative form. The cor anglais itself is to a great extent merely a symbol; much the same remarks apply, in varying degrees, to solo instru-

---

[1] It might perhaps be as well to make it clear that here I am using the adjective 'symphonic' to denote the characteristics of what is by universal consent considered to be the most important and typical movement of the classical form, namely the first. Consequently what has been said above does not necessarily apply to, say, a slow lyrical movement which, in the ordinary symphony, plays the part of a foil and contrast to the other movements and can, indeed, be said to embody the opposite principles. In Borodin's Second Symphony in B minor, for example, one finds that the cor anglais is employed in the slow movement but in none of the other three movements—a fact that constitutes a striking tribute to the great Russian master's unfailing instinct for style, besides bearing out the truth of what has been said above.

ments in general. Into the ideal symphonic orchestra in fact, like the animals into Noah's ark, the wind instruments enter two by two, or three by three if you will, but not one by one. Solo instruments, like solitary human beings, are apt to become introspective, self-conscious, unsociable, as it were, and this, as I have already said, is alien to the true symphonic style.

In general one might say that, so far as orchestration is concerned, the symphonic style is averse to the picturesque, the opulent, the highly coloured, preferring rather a certain austerity, dryness, asceticism even, of instrumental means. The same applies to the harmonic idiom which, in the ideal symphony —the symphony in the mind of God, to speak Platonically—avoids as a rule the luscious, the sensuous, the impressionistic, as foreign to its nature. Similarly the thematic material which is best fitted to symphonic treatment does not generally consist in broad, sweeping melodies of large dimensions and symmetrical cast, but rather in small, pregnant motives, insignificant in themselves, which lend themselves more freely to development and transformation than themes of a more conventionally attractive type.

There is also a texture and a manner of writing

which one feels to be symphonic and another which one feels to be unsymphonic. Strict contrapuntal, or fugal, writing, for example, is felt to be opposed to the innermost character of symphonic style, which prefers a predominantly vertical and harmonic mode of thought; the reason being that the fugue and the symphony stand at opposite poles to each other and embody diametrically antagonistic principles of construction—the principles of thematic unity and of thematic diversity respectively. The fugue and the symphonic poem, despite their superficial differences are alike in that both similarly develop from a single thematic germ, whereas the true symphonic movement develops from the interaction of two or more. Anything that tends to compromise the integrity of this fundamental symphonic principle is antagonistic to the symphonic style. Corollarily, it follows that the device of linking together the several movements of a symphony into one vast whole, under the autocracy of a constantly recurring *leitmotiv*—or 'motto' theme, as it is often called—constitutes a betrayal of the innermost spirit of symphonic style. Indeed, any interchange of thematic material between the movements is alien to it, for the treatment in each movement of the thematic material proper to it should be so complete and exhaustive as to afford no scope or excuse for its introduction into another. If it is not complete and exhaustive the movement is logically and structurally imperfect, while if it is so the repetition of its material elsewhere becomes organically superfluous and rhetorical merely. In either case the result is aesthetically unsatisfactory, and the faults of most modern symphonic writing can in large part be traced to this tendency to break down the frontiers of the separate movements. The relation between the movements of the ideal symphony, in fact, should be similar to that between the city states of ancient Greece or of medieval and Renaissance Italy—parts of a whole, but self-contained, related to each other but structurally independent and autonomous. And in the same way that the decadence of the old classical civilization dates from the union of states under Alexander the Great and that of Renaissance Italy from the attempt at unification under Pope Alexander VI, so the decline of the classical symphony dates from the destruction of the autonomy of the separate movements and the introduction of the *leitmotiv* or *idée fixe*. I need hardly say that I speak from a purely formal point of view. As I have already said, no one admires the 'Symphonie Fantastique' more than I do, but the fact is that it is not so much a symphony as a gigantic symphonic poem in five movements, which is an entirely different thing. Similarly it would be absurd to deny that the intrusion of a theme from one movement into another can occasionally produce the happiest effect. The *locus classicus* of this is, of course, the recurrence in the *finale* of Beethoven's Fifth Symphony of the theme of the *scherzo*. The fact remains that isolated strokes of genius such as that cannot be regarded as legitimate precedents, and their effect is in inverse ratio to the frequency with which they occur. Certainly the extension of this method of procedure to the point reached in many modern symphonies so-called, in which the movements are often virtually indistinguishable from each other, has been wholly pernicious from a formal point of view.

Needless to say, the above attempts to define the essential characteristics of symphonic style are not to be regarded as hard-and-fast rules in any way, but are merely broad generalizations admitting of innumerable exceptions. Mozart alone could furnish an exception to almost every one of them. For example, one need look no farther than the first movement of the G minor Symphony for a great symphonic theme of *grande envergure*, and no farther than the *finale* of the C major for a great symphonic movement based on fugal principles, and so on. But Mozart, as I have already observed, is the exception to every rule that can be devised, and on the whole I think it can be said that the principles laid down above will be found to hold good in the vast majority of cases, which is as much as one can reasonably expect. And now let us consider the symphonies of Sibelius collectively, and see to what extent they conform to them.

The first thing that strikes one about Sibelius's symphonies viewed as a whole is their astonishing range and diversity. Each one is sharply differentiated from all the others; each has a definite character of its own. Similarly, within each individual symphony one finds the same strong contrast between the constituent movements. They bear a spiritual relationship to each other, but they are always formally independent, self-sufficient entities, capable of standing alone by themselves. This is largely in consequence of the composer's consistent avoidance of thematic interconnexion between the movements. It is true that in the First Symphony we find the theme of the introduction to the first movement recurring at the beginning of the last, but one can hardly say that the two movements are thematically connected, for the melody in question plays no part in the subsequent proceedings in the first movement, and only a very small one in the last. Still, it is significant to note that, after toying tentatively with this device in his First Symphony, he then resolutely discarded it and henceforth uncompromisingly maintained the structural integrity of all the separate movements. One partial exception only may be found in the Fourth Symphony, where a phrase which occurs near the end of the third movement bears a definite, though possibly accidental, resemblance to that with which the last movement begins; but as it only appears the once in each movement, and plays no thematic role in either, one cannot say that there is any real relation between the two movements.

Another striking feature of the series taken as a whole is that, starting with the full modern orchestra, complete with bass tuba and harp, Sibelius subsequently reduces his instrumental forces down practically to the level of the old classical orchestra. In this progression the Sixth, as we have already noted, provides an exception, but the momentary relaxation which this represents was not maintained in its successor. In any case, an inspection of the full score and a careful study of the way in which the accessory instruments, namely, bass clarinet and harp, are written for, shows that this seeming augmentation of resources is largely illusory. That is to say, they are employed in order to fulfil a humble function with regard to the whole and not on account of their instrumental personalities, so to speak. Apart from a brief phrase of a single bar in the first movement, anticipating the return of the principal subject, the part for the bass clarinet consists entirely in a doubling and reinforcement of the other bass instruments and in holding unobtrusive pedal notes. No opportunity is given to it for exhibiting its peculiar characteristics as a solo instrument, for indulging in the sombre monologues and soliloquies to which it is addicted in the scores of most other composers. Similarly the harp part is of the utmost reticence and discretion, consisting almost entirely of the simplest kinds of chords and arpeggios. In other words, these two intruders into the orchestral symposium of the classical symphonic orchestra are only tolerated on the strict condition that they lay aside their personalities and subordinate themselves to the demands of the texture as a whole. They are never allowed to display themselves or to become prominent in any way.

Again, from first symphony to last one finds a steady, consistent diminution in the use of contrapuntal devices, culminating in the Seventh, in which no trace of *fugato* and singularly little polyphony even of the freest kind are to be found. Finally, the whole sequence shows a progressive disinclination to employ large-scale symmetrical melodies as his thematic material, and an ever-increasing tendency to build the movements out of short and fragmentary subject-matter.

In each successive symphony, in short, one finds Sibelius continually approximating ever more closely in one respect or another, sometimes in several, and sometimes in all, to the ideal symphonic style as set forth in the preceding pages: characterized by the thematic independence of the movements, sobriety and restraint in the use of the orchestra, the absence of contrapuntal devices, and terseness and brevity of thematic material—but above and beyond all by the protean versatility, the consummate breadth of style, the wide range of thought and emotion, the unique capacity to excel in every type of formal construction, to which reference was made at the outset of the chapter. It is in the combination of all these qualities in varying degrees that the greatness of Sibelius as a symphonist primarily resides. At the same time I am only too well aware that one of the distinguishing traits of a man of genius is an uncomfortable habit of disconcerting his critics and commentators by suddenly doing exactly the opposite of what they logically expect from his previous development, and I should not be surprised in the slightest if in his Eighth Symphony, which I understand has been completed and will probably have been produced before this book sees the light, he turns his back upon his previous achievements in symphonic form and does something entirely different, which will seem to impair the validity of much that has been said in the present chapter. Should this prove to be so I would only point out that I have already allowed for such a possibility by explicitly admitting that no hard-and-fast rules can be laid down for the conduct of genius—that it is perfectly possible for a composer to write a great symphony which contradicts everything I have said above without necessarily invalidating thereby the general principles that have been advanced.

PART THREE

CONCLUSIONS

I. THE MUSIC CONSIDERED
AS A WHOLE

Few, if indeed any, modern composers have written such a vast quantity of music, in such a wide variety of forms and categories, as Sibelius has. Apart from some fifty works in manuscript or without opus number, and also a large amount of music which has disappeared or has been destroyed, the total of his numbered and published works stands at about one hundred and twenty at the time of writing, comprising eight symphonies, about thirty large choral or orchestral works and the same number of smaller ones, a hundred or so songs and as many piano pieces, incidental music to a dozen or more plays, and innumerable miscellaneous compositions of every sort and description. Consequently, in the foregoing brief survey of his art we have been compelled to confine our attention to the more important and outstanding examples of it only; to have dealt at length and in detail with each separate work would have required a volume of wellnigh encyclopedic dimensions.

Fortunately, however, it was neither necessary nor desirable to do so. One does not as a rule need to be acquainted with everything a man has written in order to arrive at a reasonably accurate estimate of his artistic achievement as a whole, which is all that has been attempted here, and in such a large output as that of Sibelius in particular it goes without saying that there are many works of minor importance which can be conveniently ignored and even some that are completely negligible.

This immense fecundity, combined with a certain unevenness of quality, has always militated strongly against Sibelius in the eyes of many superior persons who are disposed to regard these characteristics of his with the same stern disapproval as that with which eugenists regard the unsystematic, uncontrolled proliferation of the lower classes. According to them, the artist should so control his creative urge as to permit nothing unworthy to escape into existence—he should either produce a masterpiece or else remain silent.

There is undoubtedly much that is sympathetic in this point of view, in theory at least. It is certainly better to produce one healthy and intelligent offspring than a large family of weaklings and mental defectives, and better to write one good composition than a vast horde of mediocre ones. In practice, however, it does not by any means work out as one might have expected, for in the same way that the best human specimens are generally members of large families, so the greatest works of art are as a rule the fruit of immense and frequently unequal productivity on the part of their creators. A certain reckless prodigality and effortless profusion is almost invariably, in fact, one of the distinguishing traits of the great artist, and the man of small and relatively perfect output is seldom in the first rank.

The exuberant fecundity of Sibelius, then, is a positive quality, even if some of its by-products are purely negative; it is a necessary condition of the highest creative achievements, and I do not think that the proportion of indifferent works to good ones is perceptibly greater with him than with any other composer of outstanding eminence, except possibly Bach. Let any one who doubts the truth of this contention try to wade solidly through the complete works of Beethoven, Schubert, Mozart even, and he will be surprised to discover how much of their music is completely valueless.

'Granted', it may be said, 'that the greatest masters are extremely prolific, and that their level of accomplishment may frequently be somewhat unequal, yet there are certain special features in connexion with Sibelius's immense productivity that call for explanation. One accepts the fact that a composer cannot be expected to maintain the same high level consistently throughout such a large output, but one is surely at least entitled to expect that his aim and endeavour shall be consistently lofty; and the fact that Sibelius frequently condescends to write works of a frankly popular and even trivial character is exceedingly difficult to reconcile with the high claims that are put forward on his behalf. At the very least it must surely be admitted to constitute a serious failing, a weakness that reflects adversely on his work as a whole.'

This objection must be squarely faced, for there is no denying the fact that the sentiments above expressed represent the views of a considerable number of good people to whom this side of Sibelius's activities is a genuine stumbling-block in the way of their understanding and appreciation of his work. I have already dealt with one aspect of the problem in connexion with the waltzes (see p. 104), but it will be as well to go more deeply into the question here.

The idea at the back of this attitude would seem to be that in many people's minds there is a definite gulf fixed between what is detestably called 'classical' music on the one hand and 'popular' music on the other, and it is certainly true that in modern times composers have tended to separate out into two distinct categories, those of serious aims and those who seek merely to entertain. It was not always so, however. Up to the beginning of the nineteenth century and the rise of the Romantic Movement there was no such hard-and-fast distinction between the two, and the same composers were equally active in both directions, the creative and the recreative. The origin of the schism can probably be traced to the promulgation by Schopenhauer and others of such transcendental ideas as that music is 'the metaphysical to everything physical in the world, and the thing-in-itself to every phenomenon', in consequence of which the composer of serious aims came to feel it beneath his dignity merely to amuse or entertain the great public, and the degeneration of 'popular' music which took place during the latter part of the nineteenth century is a direct result of this refusal on the part of the best composers of the time to have anything to do with it, and of their abandonment of the field to unworthy practitioners. The great classical masters, on the contrary, never disdained to cultivate the humbler field of light music, and if Sibelius does not hesitate to do so whenever the spirit moves him, neither did Beethoven, Schubert, nor Mozart, as a study of their lists of works clearly shows. In doing so, in fact, he merely shows himself to be in conformity with the authentic classical tradition, which refuses to admit that there is anything inherently reprehensible in thus providing the public with innocent enjoyment and diversion. This sense of guilt and shame in the face of artistic recreation, indeed, is entirely a thing of the last century, a kind of aesthetic puritanism. The classical symphony itself, as we have already had occasion to point out, with its minuet, *scherzo*, or other form of dance movement, expressly provides for and even insists on the inclusion of an element of pure recreativeness, and Sibelius's greatness as a symphonist is due as much to his capacity for writing a good march or dance as to his powers in other directions. Corollarily, it may be said that the failure of most modern symphonists is largely a consequence of their inability or unwillingness to do so, and to a wrong-headed conception of what constitutes the dignity of art. In practically all Sibelius's essays in this category, moreover, there is a quality of pure craftsmanship and often an originality of conception that are of intrinsic value. The 'Alla Marcia' of the 'Karelia' suite, for example, is admirably constructed, de-lightfully scored, and probably altogether the best march that has been written since the 'Marche hon-groise' in the 'Damnation de Faust' of Berlioz; similarly, whatever one may think of the 'Valse triste', it cannot surely be denied that it is a work of considerable originality.

This popular side to the art of Sibelius, then, so far from being a fault, seems to me to be another positive virtue, like his immense fertility, and one of the signs of his true greatness. Most of the ills, in-deed, to which modern music is subject are the out-come of over-sophistication, the self-conscious fear of the banal and the commonplace, the inability to relax and to be spontaneous, simple, unaffected, straightforward, unpretentious. Even many of those who are sufficiently intelligent to be well aware of this are unable to escape from their inhibitions. The desperate attempts, for example, of so many modern composers to write 'popular' music—generally along the lines of jazz—are painfully laboured, mannered, and unnatural, achieving cheapness without popu-larity, vulgarity without success, and appealing only to the depraved palates of a sophisticated few. Sibe-lius, on the contrary, achieves genuine popularity and success without ever seeming to seek it. And if he is probably the most austere and inaccessible of living composers in some of his works, he is at the same time the most familiar and accessible in others, while between these two extremes there lie compositions of every conceivable gradation and variety of appeal.

Sibelius, in fact, has provided a satisfactory answer to the question which has been debated so solemnly and for so long by philosophers, aestheticians, and art critics, namely, whether the artist should create for his own personal satisfaction like Flaubert, for an ideal audience of a 'happy few' as urged by Stendhal, primarily for his own countrymen in accordance with the doctrines of the nationalists, for Mr. Newman's hypothetical 'average intelligent music-lover', or for the ordinary man in the street or simple peasant as Tolstoy would have him do; and he has solved the problem by writing music for all of them, of each kind, at different times, in different works.

This wide diversity of intellectual and emotional appeal is achieved by means of a style of quite remarkable breadth and catholicity; melodic writing which ranges from clear-cut symmetrical tunes of a comparatively obvious kind on the one hand, to small incisive motives of a few notes only on the other; a harmonic idiom at times of the utmost simplicity and directness, and at others of great daring and singularity; rhythms now primitive, dynamic, insistent, now highly refined, sensitive, subtle; formal organizations comprehending both the most elementary and straightforward, the most complex and intricate kinds; and an instrumental palette disposing of every shade of tone-colour from the darkest and most sombre to the brightest and most luminous, sometimes employed with the utmost restraint and economy, and sometimes with the utmost lavishness and prodigality. At the same time, his command of these immense natural resources renders it unnecessary for him ever to go to violent extremes in any single direction. One does not find anywhere in his music the melodic distortions, the harmonic excesses, the rhythmical obsessions, the formal complexities, the instrumental perversities, that are, one or other and sometimes all, to be found in the work of most modern composers; his utterance is consistently natural, direct, unforced. Finally, and perhaps most important of all, behind this breadth of thought and catholicity of style one always feels a fundamental unity, and the presence of a definite personality. Indeed, there is no music in the world more intensely personal than the music of Sibelius, yet none has fewer recognizable mannerisms than his. It is true that a close student of his work can point to certain stylistic peculiarities which are to be found in it—a constantly recurring triplet figuration in his melodic writing, a fondness for introducing a phrase with a held note beginning on an off-beat, a marked predilection for long, winding passages for strings alone, with repeated notes, *flautato*, a distinctively individual disposition of the wood-wind *ensemble*, and so forth—but on the whole such idiosyncrasies are few and minute in comparison with those of most modern composers, and cannot alone be held responsible for the impression of a powerful personality which transpires through every bar in a way which it is impossible to define in any technical terms. Indeed, one often feels it most strongly in passages which, to all outward seeming, might have been written by any one —in little fragments of scale passages, for example, or simple sequences of common chords. His originality, in fact, lies in the thought, not in the means employed; and while most of his eminent contemporaries achieve a personal utterance by means of selection and restriction of means, Sibelius achieves it through comprehensiveness and inclusion. The consequence is that, whereas most other modern composers can be—and are—easily imitated, Sibelius cannot be; his individuality is independent of formulas and methods of procedure.

Despite the fact that it is at first sight somewhat difficult to distinguish any definite or consistent line of development and progress from first to last in Sibelius's chronological catalogue, his work nevertheless, on close study, like that of so many artists, reveals three distinct phases, or, more accurately perhaps, personalities: the first of which one may call the romantic and national, the second the eclectic and cosmopolitan, and the third the classic and universal. The first is primarily characterized by symphonic poems and choral works based upon, or related to in some way, episodes in the *Kalevala* or Finnish mythology in general, the last by the symphonies, and the intermediate one by miscellaneous compositions of every kind. And although these three more or less distinct personalities do not give place to each other but are developed side by side throughout his career, each of them is in the ascendant at different periods of it. A late work such as 'Tapiola', for example, belongs to the first, and another late work, the incidental music to 'The Tempest', to the second; but the fact remains that on the whole the romantic national compositions preponderate in the first period of his creative activity, the cosmopolitan and eclectic works in the second, and the symphonies in the third. It is interesting to observe, moreover, that this sequence corresponds fairly closely with three definite phases in the composer's life: the first during which he resided principally in Helsingfors and became a national figure, the second in which he travelled extensively abroad and attained a European reputation, and the third coinciding with the period of seclusion in Järvenpää. The order of chapters in the present study, it will be noted, has been designed so as to preserve and emphasize this sequence.

The most significant feature of the music of the first phase or personality consists in the fact that with it the North becomes fully articulate for the first time in the history of music. Up till then, largely as a result of the predominating role played by the Mediterranean countries, and particularly Italy, in the development of forms and idioms, music had always been overwhelmingly Latin in character, even in the work of such strongly Teutonic masters as Bach and Beethoven. Not until the nineteenth century was well advanced could it even be said that a specifically German musical idiom had come into existence, and even then the far North still remained musically inarticulate. Schumann, on hearing Niels Gade's 'Ossian' for the first time, ventured to predict that with this work the long overdue participation of the northern races in the European concert had begun, but in truth the Danish composer was too strongly under the influence of Mendelssohn, and consequently of semi-Italianate classicism, to achieve an authentically Nordic form of art. Later, certainly, in the music of Grieg, a distinctively northern mentality and accent can be discerned, but the extremely narrow limits within which his talents were confined precluded him from realizing anything more than a very partial, inadequate, and superficial aspect of the wide range of possibilities for musical expression afforded by the northern spirit. The music of Grieg is all a kind of musical picture post-card, in fact, with peasants in picturesque local costumes dancing against a background of unnaturally blue fiords and snow-clad mountains. The music of the Russian masters, again, is eastern rather than northern in geographical character and atmosphere, and Wagner, in his attempt to capture, in the 'Ring', something of the qualities expressed in Scandinavian folk-lore and mythology, fails to transcend the merely Teutonic. Such things as 'Kullervo' and 'En Saga', however, could not possibly have been written by a composer of any southern race, or even by one of other than Baltic provenance; with these works, in fact, a whole world of infinite possibilities is opened up to musical exploitation—a vein of melody, of harmony, of rhythm, of orchestration, not so much new, perhaps, as neglected hitherto by composers. For the first time the potentialities of what may be called the lower end of the tonal spectrum are thoroughly explored. Until then the aim in scoring had always been, and was for some time to remain, in the direction of ever greater brilliance and sonority; the more garish the scoring the greater was the orchestrator's reputation. Brahms, indeed, is perhaps the only composer of eminence before Sibelius deliberately and consciously to have recourse to half-shades and subdued colour-schemes, and he has always been violently abused for doing so, but his experiments in this direction were timid and tentative in comparison with those of Sibelius. And though it would certainly be a mistake, as I have already said, to imagine that Sibelius confines himself entirely to such dark and sombre effects of tone-colour, or even that they noticeably predominate in his music viewed as a whole, it is nevertheless true that his innovations in this respect constitute the element of primary value and importance in the work of his first period.

This northern and largely national phase of Sibelius's creative activity is in the ascendant until about the turn of the century. It never entirely disappears, however, and at least one of the best works of his middle period, 'Luonnotar', and one of the best of his later period, 'Tapiola', belong essentially to this category. The fact remains that the decade 1900–10 presents on the whole a very different aspect or physiognomy from the preceding one, as a study of his chronological catalogue clearly shows, consisting in a conspicuous decrease in the number and importance of the more predominantly nationalistic and Nordic works, and a corresponding increase in the number and importance of those which I have loosely designated as cosmopolitan and eclectic—loosely, because there is a sense in which such works can also be considered national, though in a different way from those of the first category, as representing, in fact, the Swedish side of the composer's personality. Cosmopolitanism and eclecticism, indeed, have always, paradoxically enough, been a racial characteristic of the Scandinavian peoples. The Latins in general, it may be observed, do not readily assimilate themselves to alien surroundings; wherever they go they take their national habits and language with them, as may be seen to-day in America or in the French and Italian colonies in London. The northerner, on the other hand, generally becomes entirely denationalized, and quickly identifies himself with his surroundings. A medieval chronicler, Geoffrey Malaterra, writing of the northern peoples, calls them 'cujuslibet rei simulatrix'—given to imitation of every kind—and wherever the Norman invaders went, whether to France, England, Sicily, or anywhere else, one invariably finds them adopting the language and national sentiments of the countries in which they settled and of the various peoples with which they came into contact. This capacity for assimilation and adaptability has always been particularly characteristic of the Swedes, and Sibelius, who, as we have already seen, is by extraction and upbringing a Swede just as much as, if not more than, he is a Finn, in accommodating himself with ease to every variety of racial tradition in his incidental music and numerous other works, principally of his middle period, only shows himself to be a typical Swede. We have already had occasion to draw attention to this duality of Finn and Swede in speaking of the composer's personality; it is an equally striking feature of his art.

This characteristically assimilative propensity is, of course, a source of weakness in many ways; it is the chief fault of much Swedish art and of practically all Swedish music in particular, and it is true that in the works of Sibelius which belong to this category one occasionally feels a certain colourless neutrality and eclecticism which are in curiously striking contrast to the originality and sturdy independence of outlook which one finds in the rest of the music. At the same time this characteristic can also be a source of strength. In the same way that the transfusion of northern blood has frequently, in the history of the past, given a fresh lease of life and energy to the rest of Europe, so we find much the same thing happening to-day in the domain of art. Modern European drama owes whatever vitality it possesses to two northerners, Ibsen and Strindberg—the fathers of realism and expressionism respectively—and from the North also has come the finest, indeed the only, architecture of modern times, of which the fruitful and stimulating influence is to be seen at work in every country at the present day. And just as the primary quality of the magnificent Town Hall at Stockholm of Ragnar Ostberg consists in its eclecticism of style, its triumphant revivification and revitalization of southern European architectural motives, so in such works as the Violin Concerto, the String Quartet, the 'In Memoriam' of Sibelius one finds a similar rejuvenation of languishing classical motives, an infusion of fresh life and vigour into effete traditions, which is primarily attributable to his strain of northern adaptability and Swedish eclecticism.

But in spite of the greatness of his achievement in these two diametrically opposite directions—that of romantic Finnish nationalism on the one hand, of cosmopolitan Swedish traditionalism on the other— there can be little doubt that, everything considered, Sibelius's greatest achievement lies in his symphonies, which constitute the most outstanding landmarks in the third phase of his productivity. In the other two categories it is conceivable that he may be occasionally equalled by other modern composers—although 'Luonnotar' and 'Tapiola' in the first and the Violin Concerto and the String Quartet in the second seem to me, in their different ways, to be unsurpassed in contemporary music— but there is nothing in modern symphonic literature that can be placed by the side of Sibelius's achievement in this direction. I would even venture farther and say that the symphonies of Sibelius represent the highest point attained in this form since the death of Beethoven.

This, I know, is a high claim to make, but I do not think that it is as high—or, consequently, as disputable—as it may perhaps seem to be at first sight, the truth of the matter being that the whole trend of music during the last century or so has been in the opposite direction to that represented by the symphonic ideal. Not that it is necessarily any the worse for that, I hasten to add; but simply that the symphonic style was not adapted to the attainment of the particular ends which most composers of the nineteenth century had in view. Symphony, as we have already observed, is the classical style *par excellence*, and music, for better or for worse—and quite possibly for neither—has for the last hundred years been in essence romantic, with all that this much misused but nevertheless indispensable adjective implies: namely, amongst other things, the predominance of sensation over intellect, of colouristic over linear interest, of expressiveness over formal balance and proportion. The inevitable result has been that in most of the symphonies written during the last century the integrity of the style has been corrupted by the intrusion of elements alien to its nature. The symphonies of the great Romantics, for example, the 'Fantastique' and the 'Harold en Italie' of Berlioz, the 'Faust' and the 'Dante' of Liszt—whatever their merits considered simply as music, are not symphonies at all, but symphonic poems in disguise; and the vast majority of modern symphonies so called are neither one nor the other, but sterile compromises between two antagonistic principles, chimerical hybrids engendered by the union of different species. The D minor Symphony of César Franck, for example, with its 'cyclic' form, its long-winded, cloying melodies which permit of no fruitful developments, its slimy chromatic harmonies and abuse of canonic devices, is the unapproachable model of everything that should be avoided in symphonic writing; and it will be found that the symphonies of such composers as Bruckner and Mahler, Tchaikovsky and Elgar, and indeed of every important practitioner of the form in modern times, sin in one or more crucial respects against the symphonic spirit—either through the employment of the device of the thematic interconnexion of all or some of the movements, through the excessive sensuousness of harmony, melody, or orchestration, or through formal invertebracy and redundance, and sometimes through all of them.

Sibelius, in fact, alone in modern times, has preserved inviolate the purity and integrity of the true
symphonic style.

There remain to be considered the symphonies of
what is often called, for the sake of convenience,
the neo-classic school, of which the most important
members are Schubert, Mendelssohn, Schumann,
and Brahms. The first-named stands in a place by
himself. Schubert must be conceded to have been
potentially a great symphonist; the 'Unfinished'
clearly shows this, but it remains a lovely torso. For
the rest the C major Symphony unquestionably
contains superb music, but in form it is undeniably
diffuse and incoherent, while none of his earlier
essays in the form is of prime importance. As for
Mendelssohn and Schumann, there are few critics
to-day who would be prepared to maintain that
either of them was a symphonist of the first rank,
whatever may be the value of their respective
achievements in other directions, and in the future
there are likely to be even fewer. It is enough to say
that both alike were essentially romantic, lyrical
miniaturists, with no real sense of form on a large
scale, incapable of conceiving thematic material of
a genuinely symphonic order, or of developing it
symphonically even if they had been able to do so.

The same criticisms apply to a very great extent to the symphonies of Brahms also. Although he certainly possessed a keener sense of the nature of the true symphonic style than any of his contemporaries or immediate predecessors and successors, and consequently avoided the errors and pitfalls into which most of them fell, the fact remains that, like them, he was essentially a romantic at heart. He achieved the symphonic style through a kind of self-immolation. One always feels with him, in the symphonies, a sense of effort and constraint, a continual striving after an ideal that was foreign to his innermost being. He was not a symphonist by natural aptitude or inclination, in fact, and on the whole this is true of all the most eminent German composers of the nineteenth century and of modern times. The Teutonic genius in music, indeed, as in everything else, is pre-eminently lyric, contemplative, philosophic, and fundamentally opposed to the dramatic, the heroic, the epic, which constitute the essence of the symphonic style. The old academic theory of the superiority of the Teuton over all other races in respect of large-scale constructive capacity is simply a myth based upon one or two great exceptions such as Beethoven; but Beethoven was no more a typical German than Goethe was, and it is the attempt on the part of German composers to emulate the great, but for them fatally misleading, example of Beethoven, and the obsession of the colossal, that are primarily responsible for all the worst faults of German music since his time. The real Bruckner, for instance, is at heart a charming Schubertian lyricist; the real Mahler is not the ambitious architect of the vast symphonies, but the composer of delicate and exquisite songs such as the 'Kindertotenlieder', other settings of poems by Ruckert, and the 'Knabe Wunderhorn' cycle. German music, in fact, is primarily rooted in song—romantic song—and consequently in spirit is fundamentally opposed to the symphonic style.

The truth is, therefore, that the Germans are in reality the last people in the world who have the right to arrogate to themselves, as they do, the supremacy over all other races in symphonic music, and to claim that they alone possess the secret of musical construction on a large scale. It is the one thing of which, as a race, they are fundamentally incapable, and this makes their patronizing attitude towards the symphonies of Sibelius particularly laughable. Attention has already been drawn in the second chapter of this book to the dictum of Herr Niemann to the effect that Sibelius's employment of

short-winded, Nordic, national, thematic material
prevents him from attaining to the 'monumentality
and concentration of form, the organic and logical
inner development and proportion' which are the
hall-mark of 'the true symphonic creations of the
West'—by which, of course, is meant Germany.
Now, quite apart from the entirely mistaken notion
that the thematic material of Sibelius's symphonies
is in any way nationalistic, the criticism shows a
complete misunderstanding of the nature of the
form. It is true that most of his themes are short-
winded, but that is precisely one of the reasons why
he is a great symphonist—it is a characteristic of
practically all the finest symphonies that have yet
been written. And it is precisely the long-winded,
Teutonic thematic material of the German symphonists of the nineteenth century that prevents
them from attaining to the monumentality and concentration of form, &c., which are the hall-mark of
the true symphonic creations of the Finnish master.
This is certainly the case with Brahms, who said
himself once, in an unguarded moment, that whenever he wished to compose he thought of some
German folk-song and then his theme presented
itself to him. The consequence was a complete lack
of that variety of mood and breadth of style which

are the prime requisite of symphonic writing—the one quality on account of which all sins can be forgiven. Brahms's movements, however they are labelled, practically all seem to be *andante con moto*; he is incapable of writing either a true *allegro* or an *adagio* movement—above all a *scherzo*. He entirely lacks gaiety, verve, spontaneity, abandon, in default of which a symphony is necessarily incomplete and imperfect. For this reason alone, if for no other, despite their many admirable and sympathetic qualities—dignity and nobility of conception, sure sense of design, careful and conscientious workmanship—the symphonies of Brahms must be accounted inferior, *qua* symphonies, to those of some composers of possibly lesser stature on the whole, such as Borodin for instance, whose two symphonies, though not among the very greatest examples of the form, nevertheless reveal a surer sense of symphonic style than those of any Teutonic composer since Schubert, or for that matter of any other composer of the nineteenth century. Neither in quantity nor in intrinsic significance, however, can Borodin's symphonic achievement be compared to that of Sibelius, who stands out, therefore, as the greatest master of the symphony since the death of Beethoven.

There is, indeed, only one partial shortcoming, one gap in his otherwise all-round creative capacity, that prevents one from ranking his finest symphonies with those of the master himself. We have already observed, when dealing with the songs, that Sibelius, apart from occasional happy inspirations, is not a great lyricist; and in his symphonies one feels a lack of that very quality in which lies the greatest and indeed the only strength of his German rivals. It is significant to note that he seldom attempts to write a typical 'slow movement'. There is none in the accepted sense of the words in either the Third, Fifth, Sixth, or Seventh Symphonies; the second movement of the First is the only one in the others which could properly be said to be lyrical, and despite its undeniable beauty, it must be accounted the weakest in the work. It is certainly the least original, the least personal, and on the whole it is true to say of practically all his more lyrical moments that they verge perilously on the commonplace and the conventional. (An exception should, however, be made in favour of the lovely slow movements of the Violin Concerto and the String Quartet.)

One may freely concede, then, that there is a certain lack of warmth, of humanity, in the music of Sibelius; one will search in vain in it for anything to compare with the deep, heart-searching, slow movements of the later Beethoven, which seem to bear within them the very secret of the universe, and go far to justify the ways of God to Man. Apart from this one qualification, I do not hesitate to express my considered opinion, for what it is worth, with all due consciousness of its implications, that in no other respect can he be regarded as at all inferior even to Beethoven himself as a symphonist. I would even go farther and say that in sheer constructive mastery and intellectual power not even such consummate achievements as the first movements of the 'Eroica' and the 'Choral' can be placed above those of Sibelius's Second, Fourth, or Fifth, and not even beside the gigantic single movement of the Seventh, which seems to me to be one of the highest summits to which music has yet attained in these respects.

For this reason, quite apart from its intrinsic value, the later work of Sibelius is a highly significant symptom and an historical event of the first importance. Generally speaking, the whole history of music during the last hundred years or so has been one of idiomatic development and expansion, a progressive enrichment of every kind of tonal resource—melodic, harmonic, rhythmic, colouristic—

accompanied by a corresponding weakening and impoverishment on the formal and intellectual side of the art. The beginnings of this tendency are to be seen in the music of Bellini, Chopin, Weber, and Berlioz as clearly as its end in that of Strauss, Schönberg, Bartók, and Stravinsky. In other words, the art of these latter composers, despite its factitious appearance of novelty, is in reality nothing more than the continuation and final phase of the Romantic Movement, the end of the old rather than the beginning of the new, as it is commonly represented to be. That it is impossible to go any farther in the direction of idiomatic innovation can be almost mathematically proved; all notes of the chromatic scale have now been sounded together harmonically, every species of melodic progression, involving the widest imaginable leaps and the most unfamiliar and exotic intervals, has been employed, every conceivable instrumental combination and every possible device for the attainment of a novel shade of tone-colour have been systematically exploited. The ultimate confines of musical language have been reached, and its remotest possibilities have been explored. There is obviously nothing further to be done in the direction of idiomatic expansion, short of the adoption of third or quarter tones, and there is no reason to believe that any fruitful development of this kind will take place in our day, if ever.

On the other hand, however, there is nothing in the music of the last hundred years which can be compared with that of Bach, Mozart, or Beethoven, as regards depth of intellectual content or formal subtlety and complexity; and while most modern composers still continue desperately seeking for some hitherto unexploited resource, some thrill or sensation not previously experienced, Sibelius, almost alone among them, has gone in the opposite direction. In all his later work one finds a deliberate avoidance of anything in the nature of idiomatic novelty or experiment for its own sake, together with a refinement and intricacy of form which are only paralleled in the art of the great classics.

It is true, of course, that within the last few years an increasing number of composers have come to realize that a new departure of this kind was not merely desirable but imperatively necessary, if music was to emerge from the hopeless *impasse* in which it was confined, but it is not enough to realize the fact consciously. As M. André Gide rightly observes in an essay on the new classicism in French literature, 'ne devient pas classique qui veut—les vrais classiques sont ceux qui le sont malgré eux, ceux qui le sont sans le savoir', and the self-conscious neo-classicism of the later Stravinsky, Casella, and many others is hopelessly sterile because it is artificial and *voulu*—the outcome of deliberation, calculation, and the desire to set a new fashion. Mr. Mansell Jones, in his *Tradition and Barbarism*, a study of the new classicism, writes that in France it is becoming a little dated to be rigidly anti-romantic, and that there is already talk of neo-romanticism. Since the one criticism that such composers as those mentioned above cannot endure is that they are slightly dated, somewhat old-fashioned, we can be fairly certain that this loudly trumpeted neo-classical movement in modern music is likely to be of short duration—if, indeed, it is not already over by the time these lines appear in print. Certainly nothing that it has so far produced is of permanent aesthetic value, and it is highly entertaining to observe that the one composer of modern times who actually has achieved a genuinely spontaneous, unconscious, classic art of the first importance, namely Sibelius, should pass entirely unnoticed and disregarded by the adherents of the movement.

The chief significance, then, of Sibelius's course of development, viewed in broad outline, is that

beginning as a romantic with more or less pro-
nounced national leanings, and passing through a
transition period of eclectic cosmopolitanism, he
ends up as a supporter of the classical tradition;
after being a pioneer, an explorer of new paths in the
works of his first period, he comes back in the end
to the great high-road of musical art. In his early
work the emotional, the colouristic, the expressive
elements predominate, and the formal and intellectual ones are in comparative abeyance. With the
growth and development of his individuality, however, his style gradually undergoes a complete
change; the rich and elaborate orchestration of the
early works is replaced by an extreme sobriety
and restraint in the use of instrumental means, the
massive, rough-hewn harmonies are clarified and
attenuated, the sharply defined and immediately
arresting themes give way to melodic fragments,
sometimes the merest wisps of scale passages and
sequences, unimportant in themselves, which only
acquire significance as a result of the treatment to
which they are subjected, and of the general context and surroundings in which they are placed.
In the music of his later period, as I have already
said, there are absolutely no individual stylistic
features whatsoever, yet no music is more pro-

foundly individual, and this is the essence of classicism. To quote M. André Gide once more: 'Le triomphe de l'individualisme et le triomphe du classicisme se confondent. Or le triomphe de l'individualisme est dans le renoncement à l'individualité. . . . Les peintres et les littérateurs' (the musicians also) 'que nous louangeons le plus aujourd'hui ont une manière; le grand artiste classique travaille à n'avoir pas de manière; il s'efforce vers la banalité. . . . Et chose admirable, c'est ainsi qu'il devient le plus personnel.'

Together with this sobriety and restraint of idiom, this impersonality of style, we find a refinement and complexity of form which have no parallel in modern music, and can only be compared to those of the posthumous quartets and latest piano sonatas of Beethoven. There is, indeed, a more than superficial resemblance between the later works of Beethoven and those of Sibelius, for the latter's discarding in his later symphonies of the old formal convention of two main themes or groups of themes out of which the movement is constructed is to a great extent only the application to symphonic writing of the revolutionary formal innovations introduced by Beethoven in his last quartets and sonatas, but which he did not live long

enough to apply to large-scale orchestral compositions.[1]

In a purely technical sense, therefore—from the
point of view of formal structure—it is true to say
that in his later work Sibelius takes up music where
Beethoven laid it down. Even in his early work,
however, it is important to note that, romantic in
spirit though it is, it bears no trace whatever of the
influence of the great romantic composers themselves—the art of Weber, of Berlioz, of Chopin, of
Liszt, has had no effect, no repercussion, on that of
Sibelius. His entire art, in fact, follows on straight
from that of Beethoven, without any intermediary
influence of any kind; one can pass from one to the
other without feeling that there is an intervening gap
of a century. Indeed, there is less feeling of strangeness in passing from Beethoven to Sibelius than
from Beethoven to Berlioz. The latter opens up a
new world, the former recognizably belongs to the
same one.

It is this fact that gives the peculiar quality to all

[1] It might also be pointed out, as a matter of historical interest, that
Sibelius's method of construction in his symphonies is often strikingly
analogous to that of the early pre-Haydn symphonists of the Mann-
heim school who, in the words of the German critic, Carl Nef (*Ge-
schichte der Symphonie*, 1921), 'begnügten sich verschiedene Motive
von nicht zu sehr kontrastirender Art nebeneinander zu stellen und
in reizvoller Abwechselung aufeinander folgen zu lassen'.

his work; it is as if the last hundred years had not existed, as if the entire Romantic Movement so called were only a vast parenthesis containing much of value and interest which is nevertheless essentially irrelevant in respect of the history of music as a whole—a bypath or side-track in which may be found much that is admirable in itself, but which leads nowhere save into the morass in which most modern composers are still floundering. Above all, however, is it significant that Sibelius would seem to be practically the only modern composer—certainly the only one of his generation—who has neither been influenced by Wagner nor, what amounts to very much the same thing, reacted violently against him. The ferocious anti-Wagnerianism of Debussy, for example, is in itself highly suspicious, and a most eloquent tribute to the potent wizardry of the master of Bayreuth; one does not need to be told by his biographers that at heart Debussy had always a secret admiration and affection for the music of Wagner—the fact is clearly written in every bar of his music, and much the same may be said of most of those who fulminate so violently against it. They detest it because they cannot get away from it, in fact. Sibelius, on the contrary, does not detest Wagner for the very good reason that he has never loved him. Not even when, as a young man, he visited Bayreuth during the height of the Wagnerian cult in the early 'nineties, did Wagner mean anything to him at all, one way or the other; and the proof of this is to be found in the fact that it is impossible to lay one's finger on a single phrase in his entire work which one could attribute to the influence of Wagner, or one which would not have been exactly the same even if Wagner had never lived. I doubt very much whether there is any other composer of the last seventy years or so of whom this could be said, and it can be no mere coincidence that the one modern composer who has thus entirely escaped the influence of Bayreuth should be the one whose achievement, I firmly believe, will prove to have been the greatest of modern times. For whatever one's own personal reaction to the music of Wagner may be, it cannot, I think, be denied that his influence on other composers and on music in general has been wholly disastrous.

The influence of Sibelius, on the contrary, which is now gradually beginning to make itself felt, whatever may be the intrinsic aesthetic value of his achievement, can only be salutary and beneficial, for his art is based upon the same fundamental, immutable, and ever-fruitful principles that have inspired the great art of the past and are equally destined to inspire that of the future. Sibelius has triumphantly disproved the belief that the idioms and methods of procedure which have served so many generations of composers have now become exhausted; almost alone at the present time he has conclusively shown, what most people had legitimately begun to doubt, that it is still just as possible as it ever was to say something absolutely new, vital, and original, without having to invent a new syntax, a new vocabulary, a new language, in order to do so. Sibelius, in fact, reveals a fresh and unsuspected beauty in the old, whereas most modern composers seek to discover a familiar beauty in the new.

There are many great artists, differing from each other widely in other ways, who are alike in this, that by virtue of the very unsurpassable perfection of their achievements they are apt to engender in their successors a feeling of profound discouragement and finality. One feels that they have exhausted all the possibilities they had opened up, and that there is nothing left for those who come after them. Such are Bach, Mozart, Wagner, Chopin, Delius. Others there are, however, such as Beethoven, Berlioz, Liszt, Moussorgsky, who suggest and in-

spire as much as they themselves actually achieve.
And Sibelius is of this number. Over and above his
actual tangible donation he gives us a sense of
liberation, fresh hopes, and new energies with
which to realize them. He has cut a path through the
selva oscura wherein most modern musicians have
gone so hopelessly astray, and it is, I think, particularly significant to note that the greatest admirers
of his work, in this country at least, are to be found,
not among his contemporaries, strictly speaking,
but in the ranks of the younger generation. There
could be no fairer omen for the future. Curiously
prophetic and applicable to Sibelius, indeed, are the
words of his compatriot, the nameless Finnish poet
of ancient days who composed the lines with which
the great national epic, the *Kalevala*, concludes:

> I have shown the way to singers,
> Showed the way, and broke the tree-tops,
> Cut the branches, shown the pathways.
> This way therefore leads the pathway,
> Here the path lies newly opened,
> Widely open for the singers,
> For the young, who now are growing,
> For the rising generation.

II. COMPLETE LIST OF WORKS

A. *WITH OPUS NUMBERS*

Opus	Title	Publisher	Date
1.	Five Christmas Songs	*W.*	
2.	'Romance and Epilogue', for violin and piano	*U.*	1890
3.	'Arioso' (Runeberg), for voice and string orchestra	*W.*	1893
4.	String Quartet in B flat major	*MS.*	1890
5.	Six Impromptus for piano	*B. & H.*	1890
6.	'Cassation', for small orchestra	*MS.*	1895
7.	'Kullervo', symphony for soli, chorus, and orchestra	*MS.*	1892
8.	Incidental music to 'Ödlan' (Lybeck), for orchestra	*MS.*	1909
9.	'En Saga', tone-poem for orchestra	*B. & H.*	1892
10.	'Karelia', overture for orchestra	*B. & H.*	1893
11.	'Karelia', suite for orchestra:	*B. & H.*	1893
	(i) Intermezzo		
	(ii) Ballade		
	(iii) Alla Marcia		
12.	Sonata in F major for piano	*B. & H.*	1891
13.	Seven songs of Runeberg:	*B. & H.*	1891
	(i) 'Neath the Fir-trees		
	(ii) A Kiss's Hope		
	(iii) The Heart's Morning		
	(iv) Spring is flying		
	(v) The Dream		
	(vi) To Frigga		
	(vii) The young Sportsman		

Opus	Title	Publisher	Date
14.	'Rakastava' ('The Lover'), suite for strings and drums:	*B. & H.*	1893
	(i) Rakastava, the Lover		
	(ii) The Way of the Lover		
	(iii) Good Night, my Beloved—Farewell		
15.	'Skogsrået' (Rydberg), melodrama for recitation, piano, horns, and strings	*MS.*	1894
16.	'Spring Song' ('La Tristesse du Printemps'), for orchestra	*B. & H.*	1891
17.	Seven songs:	*B. & H.*	1894
	(i) And I questioned then no further (Runeberg)		
	(ii) Slumber (Tavaststjerna)		
	(iii) Enticement (Tavaststjerna)		
	(iv) Astray (Tavaststjerna)		
	(v) The Dragon-fly (Levertin)		
	(vi) To Evening (Forsman)		
	(vii) Driftwood (Calamnius)		
18.	Six part-songs for male voices *a cappella*:	*B. & H.*	1895
	(i) Sortunut ääni (Kanteletar)		
	(ii) Terve kuu (Kalevala)		
	(iii) Venematka (Kalevala)		
	(iv) Saarella (Kanteletar)		
	(v) Metsämiehen Laulu (Kivi)		
	(vi) Sydämeni Laulu (Kivi)		
19.	'Impromptu', 'Thou who guidest the Stars' (Rydberg), for female chorus and orchestra	*B. & H.*	1902
20.	'Malinconia', for 'cello and piano	*B. & H.*	1902

Opus	Title	Publisher	Date
21.	Hymn 'Natus in Curas', for male voices *a cappella*	B. & H.	1897
22.	Four 'Legends' for orchestra:		1893–5
	(i) Lemminkäinen and the Maiden	MS.	
	(ii) Lemminkäinen in Tuonela	MS.	
	(iii) The Swan of Tuonela	B. & H.	
	(iv) The Return of Lemminkäinen	B. & H.	
23.	Cantata for the year 1897, for mixed chorus *a cappella*	W.	1897
24.	Ten Pieces for piano:	B. & H.	1895
	(i) Impromptu		
	(ii) Romance in A flat		
	(iii) Caprice		
	(iv), (v) Two Miniatures Romance and Waltz		
	(vi) Idyll		
	(vii) Andantino		
	(viii) Nocturne		
	(ix) Romance in D flat		
	(x) Barcarolle		
25.	'Scènes Historiques' I, suite for orchestra:	B. & H.	1899
	(i) All' Overtura		
	(ii) Scène		
	(iii) Festivo		
26.	'Finlandia', tone-poem for orchestra	B. & H.	1899
27.	Incidental music to 'King Christian II' (Adolf Paul), suite for orchestra:	B. & H.	1898
	(i) (*a*) Élégie, (*b*) Musette, (*c*) Minuet, (*d*) Fool's Song		
	(ii) (*a*) Nocturne, (*b*) Serenade		
	(iii) Ballad		

Opus	Title	Publisher	Date
28.	'Sandels' (Runeberg), improvisation for male voices and orchestra	MS.	1898
29.	'Snöfrid' (Rydberg), improvisation for recitation, chorus, and orchestra	H.	1900
30.	'Islossningen' (Topelius), improvisation for recitation, male voice chorus, and orchestra	MS.	1899
31.	'Song of the Athenians' (Rydberg), for men's and boys' voices, horn septet, and percussion	B. & H.	1899
32.	'The Origin of Fire' ('Ukko the Fire-maker') (Kalevala), for baritone, male voice chorus, and orchestra	B. & H.	1902
33.	'The Ferryman's Brides' (Oksanen), for baritone or mezzo-soprano and orchestra	B. & H.	1897
34.	Eight little pieces for piano:	B. & H.	1916

    (i) Waltz
    (ii) Dance Air
    (iii) Mazurka
    (iv) Humorous
    (v) Drollery
    (vi) Reverie
    (vii) Pastoral Dance
    (viii) The Harper

| 35. | Two Songs: | B. & H. | 1904 |

    (i) Jubal (Josephson)
    (ii) Theodore (Gripenberg)

| 36. | Six songs: | B. & H. | 1898 |

    (i) Black Roses (Josephson)
    (ii) But my Bird is long in homing (Runeberg)

Opus	Title	Publisher	Dat
	(iii) Tennis at Trianon (Fröding)		
	(iv) Ingalill (Fröding)		
	(v) March Snow (Wecksell)		
	(vi) The Diamond (Wecksell)		
37.	Five songs:	B. & H.	1895
	(i) The first Kiss (Runeberg)		
	(ii) Berceuse (Topelius)		
	(iii) Sunrise (Hedberg)		
	(iv) Was it a Dream? (Wecksell)		
	(v) The Tryst (Runeberg)		
38.	Five songs:	B. & H.	1902
	(i) Autumn Night (Rydberg)		
	(ii) On a Balcony by the Sea (Rydberg)		
	(iii) Night (Rydberg)		
	(iv) The Harper and his Son (Rydberg)		
	(v) I would I were dwelling (Fröding)		
39.	Symphony No. 1 in E minor, for orchestra	B. & H.	1899
40.	'Pensées Lyriques' for piano:	B. & H.	1915
	(i) Valsette		
	(ii) Chant sans paroles		
	(iii) Humoresque		
	(iv) Menuetto		
	(v) Berceuse		
	(vi) Pensée melodique		
	(vii) Rondoletto		
41.	'Kyllikki', three lyric pieces for piano	B. & H.	1904
42.	'Romance' in C major, for strings	B. & H.	1903

Opus	Title	Publisher	Date
43.	Symphony No. 2 in D major, for orchestra	B. & H.	1902
44.	Incidental music to 'Kuolema' (Järnefelt)	B. & H.	1903
45.	Two pieces for orchestra:	B. & H.	1910
	(i) The Dryads		
	(ii) Dance Intermezzo		
46.	Incidental music to 'Pelléas et Mélisande' (Maeterlinck), suite for small orchestra:	S.	1905
	(i) At the Castle Gate		
	(ii) Mélisande		
	(iii) On the Sea-shore		
	(iv) A Spring in the Park		
	(v) The three blind Sisters		
	(vi) Pastorale		
	(vii) Mélisande at the Spinning-wheel		
	(viii) Entr'acte		
	(ix) The Death of Mélisande		
47.	Concerto in D minor, for violin and orchestra	S.	1903
48.	'The Captive Queen', ballad for chorus and orchestra	S.	?
49.	'Pohjola's Daughter', symphonic fantasia for orchestra	S.	?
50.	Six songs:	S.	1905
	(i) A Song of Spring (Fitger)		
	(ii) Longing (Weiss)		
	(iii) A Maiden yonder sings (Susman)		
	(iv) O wert thou here (Dehmel)		
	(v) The silent Town (Dehmel)		
	(vi) The Song of the Roses (Ritter)		

Opus	Title	Publisher	Date
51.	Incidental music to 'Belsazar' (Procopé), suite for small orchestra	S.	1906
	(i) Oriental Procession		
	(ii) Solitude		
	(iii) Night Music		
	(iv) Khadra's Dance		
52.	Symphony No. 3 in C major, for orchestra	S.	1908
53.	'Pan and Echo', dance intermezzo for orchestra	S.	1906
54.	Incidental music to 'Swanwhite' (Strindberg), suite for small orchestra:	S.	1908
	(i) The Peacock		
	(ii) The Harp		
	(iii) The Maiden with the Roses		
	(iv) Listen, the Robin sings		
	(v) The Prince alone		
	(vi) Swanwhite and the Prince		
	(vii) Song of Praise		
55.	'Night-ride and Sunrise', tone-poem for orchestra	S.	1907
56.	'Voces Intimae', string quartet in D minor	S.	1909
57.	Eight songs of Josephson:	S.	1909
	(i) The Snail		
	(ii) The wild Flower		
	(iii) The Millwheel		
	(iv) May		
	(v) The Tree		
	(vi) Baron Magnus		
	(vii) Friendship		
	(viii) The Elf-king		

Opus	Title	Publisher	Date
58.	Ten pieces for piano:	B. & H.	1909

    (i) Rêverie
    (ii) Scherzino
    (iii) Air varié
    (iv) The Shepherd
    (v) The Evening
    (vi) Dialogue
    (vii) Tempo di menuetto
    (viii) Fisher Song
    (ix) Serenade
    (x) Summer Song

| 59. | 'In Memoriam', funeral march for orchestra | B. & H. | 1909 |
| 60. | Two songs from Shakespeare's *Twelfth Night* | B. & H. | 1909 |

    (i) Come away, Death
    (ii) When that I was

| 61. | Eight songs: | B. & H. | 1910 |

    (i) Slow as the Colours (Tavaststjerna)
    (ii) Lapping Waters (Rydberg)
    (iii) When I dream (Tavaststjerna)
    (iv) Romeo (Tavaststjerna)
    (v) Romance (Tavaststjerna)
    (vi) Dolce far niente (Tavaststjerna)
    (vii) Idle Wishes (Runeberg)
    (viii) The Spell of Springtide (Gripenberg)

| 62. | (*a*) Canzonetta for strings | B. & H. | 1911 |
| | (*b*) Valse romantique for small orchestra | | |

Opus	Title	Publisher	Date
63.	Symphony No. 4 in A minor, for orchestra	B. & H.	1911
64.	'The Bard', tone-poem for orchestra	B. & H.	1913
65.	Two part-songs for mixed chorus *a cappella*:	B. & H.	1912
	(*a*) People of Land and of Sea		
	(*b*) Bell Melody of Berghäll-Church		
66.	'Scènes Historiques' II, suite for orchestra:	B. & H.	1912
	(i) The Chase (Overture)		
	(ii) Love-song		
	(iii) At the Draw-bridge		
67.	Three sonatinas for piano	B. & H.	1912
68.	Two rondinos for piano	U.	1912
69.	Two Serenades for violin and orchestra	B. & H.	1913
70.	'Luonnotar', tone-poem for soprano and orchestra	B. & H.	1913
71.	Incidental music to the pantomime 'Scaramouche' (Knudsen), for small orchestra	H.	1913
72.	Six songs:	B. & H.	1914
	(i) Farewell (Rydberg)		
	(ii) Orion's Girdle (Topelius)		
	(iii) The Kiss (Rydberg)		
	(iv) The Echo Nymph (Kyösti)		
	(v) The Wanderer and the Brook (Greif)		
	(vi) A Hundred Ways (Runeberg)		
73.	'The Oceanides' (Aallottaret), tone-poem for orchestra	B. & H.	1914

214

Opus	Title	Publisher	Date
74.	Four lyric pieces for piano:	*B. & H.*	1914
	(i) Eclogue		
	(ii) Soft west Wind		
	(iii) At the Dance		
	(iv) In the old Home		
75.	Five pieces for piano:	*B. & H.*	1914
	(i) When the Mountain-ash is in Flower		
	(ii) The solitary Tree		
	(iii) The Aspen		
	(iv) The Birch Tree		
	(v) The Fir Tree		
76.	Thirteen pieces for piano:	*Au.*	1914
	(i) Esquisse		
	(ii) Staccato		
	(iii) Carillon		
	(iv) Humoresque		
	(v) Consolation		
	(vi) Romanzetta		
	(vii) Affettuoso		
	(viii) Pièce enfantine		
	(ix) Arabesque (Musical Box)		
	(x) Elegiaco		
	(xi) The twin Flowers of the North		
	(xii) Capricietto		
	(xiii) Harlequinade		
77.	Two pieces for violin and small orchestra:	*H.*	1914
	(a) Laetare anima mea		
	(b) Devotion (Ab imo pectore)		
78.	Four pieces for violin (or 'cello) and piano:	*H.*	1915

215

Opus	Title	Publisher	Date
	(i) Impromptu		
	(ii) Romance		
	(iii) Religioso		
	(iv) Rigaudon		
79.	Six pieces for violin and piano:	H.	1915
	(i) Souvenir		
	(ii) Tempo di Menuetto		
	(iii) Danse caractéristique		
	(iv) Sérénade		
	(v) Dance-idyll		
	(vi) Berceuse		
80.	Sonatina for violin and piano	H.	1915
81.	Five pieces for violin and piano:	W.	1915
	(i) Mazurka		
	(ii) Rondino		
	(iii) Waltz		
	(iv) Aubade		
	(v) Menuetto		
82.	Symphony No. 5 in E flat major, for orchestra	H.	1915
83.	Incidental music to 'Jedermann' (Hoffmannsthal), for small orchestra	MS.	1916
84.	Five part-songs for male voices a cappella:	MS.	1915
	(i) Herr Lager (Fröding)		
	(ii) På berget (Fröding)		
	(iii) Ett drömackord (Fröding)		
	(iv) Evige Eros (Fröding)		
	(v) Till havs (Reuter)		
85.	Five pieces for piano:	H.	1916
	(i) Bluebells		
	(ii) The Carnation		

Opus	Title	Publisher	Date
	(iii) The Iris		
	(iv) The Snapdragon		
	(v) The Campanula		
86.	Six songs (Swedish text only):	*H.*	1916
	(i) Vår förnimmelser (Tavest-stjerna)		
	(ii) Längtan heter min arvedel (Karlfeldt)		
	(iii) Dold förening (Snoilsky)		
	(iv) Och finns det en tanke (Tavast-stjerna)		
	(v) Sångarlön (Snoilsky)		
	(vi) I systrar, I bröder (Lybeck)		
87.	(*a*) 'Impromptu' for orchestra	*H.*	1917
	(*b*) 'Humoreske' for violin and orchestra		
88.	Six songs:	*H.*	1917
	(i) The Anemone		
	(ii) The two Roses ⎫ Franzén		
	(iii) The Star-flower ⎬		
	(iv) The Primrose		
	(v) The Thornbush ⎫ Runeberg		
	(vi) The Flower ⎭		
89.	Four 'Humoresques' for violin and orchestra	*H.*	1917
90.	Six songs of Runeberg:	*B. & H.*	1917
	(i) The North		
	(ii) Your Message		
	(iii) The Morning		
	(iv) The Bird-catcher		
	(v) Summer Night		
	(vi) Who has brought you here?		

Opus	Title	Publisher	Date
91.	(a) March of the Finnish Infantry	for orchestra	*B. & H.*	1918
	(b) Scout March		*H.*	
92.	'Oma maa' (Kallio), cantata for chorus and orchestra	*MS.*	1918
93.	Cantata (Hemmer), for Abo University, for chorus and orchestra	*W.*	1919
94.	Six pieces for piano:	*H.*	1919

94. Six pieces for piano:
    (i) Dance
    (ii) Novelette
    (iii) Sonnet
    (iv) Berger et Bergerette
    (v) Mélodie
    (vi) Gavotte

95. 'Maan virsi' (Leino), cantata for chorus and orchestra   *MS.*   1920

96. Three pieces for orchestra: *H.*   1920
    (i) Valse lyrique
    (ii) Autrefois, scène pastorale
    (iii) Valse chevaleresque

97. Six 'Bagatelles' for piano: *B. & H.*   1920
    (i) Humoresque
    (ii) Song
    (iii) Little waltz
    (iv) Humorous march
    (v) Impromptu
    (vi) Humoresque

98. (a) Suite mignonne for two flutes and strings: *C.*   1921
    (i) Petite Scène
    (ii) Polka
    (iii) Epilogue

Opus	Title	Publisher	Date
	(b) Suite Champêtre for strings:	H.	
	(i) Pièce caractéristique		
	(ii) Mélodie élégiaque		
	(iii) Danse		
99.	Eight short pieces for piano:	H.	1922
	(i) Pièce humoristique		
	(ii) Esquisse		
	(iii) Souvenir		
	(iv) Impromptu		
	(v) Couplet		
	(vi) Animoso		
	(vii) Moment de valse		
	(viii) Petite marche		
100.	'Suite Caractéristique' for orchestra	H.	1922
101.	'Five Romantic Compositions' for piano:	F.	1923
	(i) Romance		
	(ii) Chant du soir		
	(iii) Scène lyrique		
	(iv) Humoresque		
	(v) Scène romantique		
102.	'Novelette' for violin and piano	H.	1923
103.	'Five Characteristic Impressions' for piano:	F.	1924
	(i) The Village Church		
	(ii) The Fiddler		
	(iii) The Oarsman		
	(iv) The Storm		
	(v) In mournful Mood		
104.	Symphony No. 6 in D minor, for orchestra	A. H.	1924
105.	Symphony No. 7 in C major, for orchestra	H.	1925

Opus	Title	Publisher	Date
106.	Five 'Danses Champêtres' for violin and piano	F.	1925
107.	'Ritual Chorus' with organ accompaniment	MS.	1925
108.	Two part-songs for male voices *a cappella*:	MS.	1925
	(i) Humoreski (Kyösti)		
	(ii) Ne pitkän (Kyösti)		
109.	Incidental music to Shakespeare's *The Tempest*, for orchestra	H.	1926

    (*a*) Prelude
    (*b*) Suite I:
        (i) The Oak-tree
        (ii) Humoreske
        (iii) Caliban's song
        (iv) The Harvesters
        (v) Canon
        (vi) Scène
        (vii) Berceuse
        (viii) Entr'acte
        (ix) The Storm
    (*c*) Suite II:
        (i) Chorus of Winds
        (ii) Intermezzo
        (iii) Dance of the Nymphs
        (iv) Prospero
        (v) Songs 1 and 2
        (vi) Miranda
        (vii) The Naiads
        (viii) Dance Episode

| 110. | 'The Song of Väino' (Kalevala), for chorus and orchestra | MS. | 1926 |

Opus	Title	Publisher	Date
111.	Two pieces for organ:	*MS.*	
	(i) Intrada		1926
	(ii) Mournful Music		1931
112.	'Tapiola', symphonic poem for orchestra	*B. & H.*	1925
113.	'Musique réligieuse' for solo voice, chorus, and organ	*MS.*	1927
114.	Five 'Esquisses' for piano:	*MS.*	1929
	(i) Landscape		
	(ii) Winter Scene		
	(iii) Forest Lake		
	(iv) Song in the Forest		
	(v) Spring Vision		
115.	Four compositions for violin and piano:	*B. & H.*	1929
	(i) Moods of the Moor		
	(ii) Tale		
	(iii) Humorous		
	(iv) The Bells (Capricietto)		
116.	Three compositions for violin and piano:	*B. & H.*	1929
	(i) Scène de Danse		
	(ii) Danse caractéristique		
	(iii) Rondeau romantique		

B. *PUBLISHED WORKS WITHOUT OPUS NUMBERS*

ORCHESTRAL

Incidental music to 'The Language of the Birds' (Adolf Paul)	*B. & H.*	1911
Academic March	*H.*	
'Tiera', tone-piece for wind instruments		1894

CHORAL

Title		Publisher	Date
Har du mod (Wecksell)	} for male chorus	B. & H.	1913
Patriotic March	} and orchestra	K.	1930
Ej med klagan (Runeberg)			1905
Drömmarne	for mixed		
Uusimaa	chorus a		
Juhlamarssi (Leino)	cappella		1912
Two Psalms			1925–7
Yks' voima (Cajander)			1898
Min rastas (Kanteletar)			1894
Veljeni (Aho)			
Jome havsfärd (Fröding)	for male		
Likhet (Runeberg)	chorus a		
Two songs (Schybergson)	cappella		1920
N. Y. Laulajat (Sola)			1929
Viborgs Sångarbröder			
'Carminalia' for boys' voices a cappella, or with piano		B. & H.	1905
Päiv ei pääse (Erkko)			
Kansakoulunmarssi	for children's		
Koulutiee (Koskenniemi)	voices a cap-		
Three songs (English) for American schools	pella		1913

SONGS

Serenad (Runeberg)			1888
Narciss (Gripenberg)			
Segeln (Ohquist)	with piano ac-		
Små flickor (Procopé)	companiment		
Sammunut			1918

WITHOUT OPUS NUMBERS

Title	Publisher	Date
PIANO PIECES		
Six Finnish Folk-songs	B. & H.	1909
Pièce romantique		1920
Till tranaden		
Kavalieren		1901
Mandolinato	H.	

RECITATION WITH PIANO

Ett ensamt skidspår (Gripenberg)

C. UNPUBLISHED WORKS WITHOUT OPUS NUMBERS

'The Maid in the Tower'; opera in one act	1896
Kröningskantat, for solo, chorus and orchestra	1895
Cantata for chorus and orchestra	1894
'Skogsrået', tone-poem for orchestra	1894
'Scène de ballet', for orchestra	1890
'Tempo di menuetto', for orchestra	
'Cortège', for orchestra	1901
'Porträtterna', for strings	
'Andante festivo', for strings	1924
'Andante lirico', for strings	
Sonata in F major, for violin and piano	1889
Suite for violin and piano	1888
Rondo for viola and piano	1895
Quartet in C major, for piano and strings	1891
Quintet in G minor, for piano and strings	1889
'Svartjukans nätter' (Runeberg), for recitation, voice, and piano trio	1888

'Necken' (Wennerberg), two songs with piano trio   1889
'Tanken' (Runeberg), duet for two sopranos with
    piano   1915

Note. There are, in addition, many early works, chiefly for chamber music combinations, which the composer no longer wishes to acknowledge.

ABBREVIATIONS OF PUBLISHERS' NAMES

A.H.	Abr. Hirsch (Stockholm)
Au.	Augener (London)
B. & H.	Breitkopf & Härtel (Leipzig)
C.	Chappell (London)
F.	Fischer (New York)
H.	Hansen (Copenhagen)
K.	Keskus (Helsingfors)
S.	Schlesinger (Berlin)
U.	Universal (Vienna)
W.	Westerlund (Helsingfors)

(*MS.*, needless to say, signifies that the work is unpublished at the time of writing. I understand that several of the works so indicated may be published in due course.)

PRINTED IN GREAT BRITAIN BY JARROLD AND SONS LTD. NORWICH